GOSPEL CONVERSATIONAL MARRIAGE

ENGAGING YOUR SPOUSE IN EVERYDAY LIFE

SAM & TONYA GREER

© 2022 Sam and Tonya Greer

All rights reserved. Except for brief excerpts for review purposes, no part of this book may be reproduced or used in any form without written permission from the author.

Scripture quotations are from the ESV® Bible (The Holy Bible, English Standard Version®), copyright © 2001 by Crossway, a publishing ministry of Good News Publishers. Used by permission. All rights reserved.

Cover Design: Trenn Carnes

ISBN: 978-0-578-97112-4

Library of Congress Control Number: 2021916740

Printed in the United States of America

First Edition 2022

Conversations

Dedication

Introductions

1. Marriage Made by Heaven
2. Marriage, What a God Idea
3. Marriage by the Book
4. Making Marriage Matter, Matters
5. Marriage and Money
6. Marriages that Can
7. Grace Moves Your Marriage from Good to Great
8. In Sickness…
9. Sex is a Good Thang
10. Social Media and Scriptural Marriage

End Notes

Dedication

Tonya and I dedicate this book to our family and friends who have invested in us through the years: Granny, Nana, Dad, Papa, Pawpaw, Pappaw, Uncle Jim, Aunt B, Chuck, Darlene, Mark, and Peggy. Jesus has taught us much through you. We thank you for your sacrifice for us as individuals and as a couple.

Introductions

Introducing Her

I grew up in the central Mississippi area with two hardworking single parents and a brother who, like most little brothers, loved to torment me. See, when you have single parents, they are gone a lot because funding two households is hard. So that left lots of time for me and the little brother to fight unsupervised. And fight we did. One fight even involved a knife being thrown by yours truly that somehow landed in the knee of the perpetrator. My little brother. But don't feel sorry for him, he totally deserved it.

You see, as much as we fought WITH each other, we would also fight to the death FOR each other. When our dad got home from a long day of work, you'd think he would tell on me and get me in big trouble. But he didn't. Instead he hid the fact that he had a giant gash in his knee that I put there. He didn't want me to get in trouble. He once nearly got expelled for threatening a boy who'd given me trouble at school. My brother totally would have knocked his lights out, but the poor kid was so scared he didn't have to. Needless to say, I never had a minute of trouble from any kid in my school ever again.

Until this day we can endlessly harass each other but no one else is allowed to. That's the thing about siblings, it's the unconditional love we all spend a lifetime seeking and many never find it. It is, however, available to ALL of us. Every. Single. One. God has a plan and a purpose for each of us. We just need to find Him and accept Him. And finding Him isn't hard. He's right there. Or right here. Wherever you are at the moment. He's there. I had always felt His presence calling me. Even as a kid, I felt Him pulling me. One time I even walked down the aisle where the pastor said I could meet Him, and I got baptized.

I led a pretty ideal life after that and somehow found myself having loads of wonderful friends in high school. It was after high school that things all kinda went downhill. All of my friends either got married and had kids early, moved far off for college, or ran off and joined the military. I really didn't know what to do with myself. I mean, I went to college and all but didn't get too far from home. I had to find a new place to fit in. What I didn't realize at the time is that I was grieving. So, I didn't make the best of decisions. In fact, I made some terrible decisions that haunt me till this day. I burned so many bridges I still cringe.

    I was pretty lonely for most of college. I didn't make a lot of friends. At least they just weren't friends that were good for me at the time. I kinda hit rock bottom my junior year and knew God was really calling me. But I put Him off because I'd made such a mess of things and I needed to get my life together first. So the downward spiral continued. Things started to improve my senior year when my bestie finished basic training and decided to transfer to The University of Southern Mississippi where I was attending. We grabbed one of the few high school friends I had not yet alienated (don't worry, I do later) and got us an apartment. We scraped together every dime we could find to survive and ate lots of Wheat Thins and Taco Bell, but we made it happen.

    My bestie, Christy, talked about this Jesus guy all the time but if you'll remember, I was still working on getting cleaned up for Him. So, I kinda drowned her out. I mean, I knew she was right and He was great and all, but He was way too great for me. I liked to go to bars and dance and maybe even drink on occasion. I was having a hard time letting that go. But she was reading these books and kept talking about how good they were and bugging me about reading them. So, I took the first in the series just to get her off my back. That particular weekend I went home to my momma. I laid across the bed and started reading one Saturday afternoon. It was *Left Behind* by Jerry B Jenkins and Tim LaHaye. So basically these two guys look at scripture and put a story together that could happen based on the info we get from the book of Revelation in the Bible. I'll never forget the first chapter. All these people have been left on earth, and their loved ones were gone. Many of them realized they had been *Left Behind*. Wow.

That really got me thinking. I was already deeply depressed and very emotionally unstable. I was even dating this guy I was absolutely crazy about, and he was so impressed with me that he once FORGOT we had plans for a date and completely stood me up. And what's worse y'all, I kept dating him! Who does that?! Talk about low self-esteem.

I digress. Wondering if I would be left behind when Jesus finally returned shook me to my core. I mean, I'd been trying to get myself right so I could go to Jesus, but the more I tried, the deeper into trouble I got myself. This flood of emotion overtook me as I was contemplating how to get good enough to go to Jesus. The only thing my body would let me do was get off my bed in my room at my momma's house and onto the floor to talk to Jesus. I literally laid out in the floor as low as I could possibly get myself and made sure He understood I was not good enough for Him yet. I told Him I didn't know when I could make this right because all I was doing was making it worse. I told Him all the reasons He wouldn't want me and I told Him I was sorry and that as hard as I was trying, it was just getting worse. And that's when it happened. Y'all, I'm not very smart, so God just had to show me. I literally felt every sin pour out of my body through my face. It was hot, it was wet, and y'all it was ugly. I still remember it so vividly. My body shook as I sobbed and the black stain from my mascara is probably still on the carpet. I know how crazy this may sound, but I saw my sin come out of my hot, wet face and land in my hands that my face was buried in. And just as if I was watching a movie, I watched God pull my hands from my face and wipe my hands clean. He then wrapped His hands around me and told me that He loved me, that my sins were covered and gone. I can't even remember how long I laid there, but I couldn't stop crying and saying, "Thank you." My burdens were lifted and gone. At that moment, I was transformed.

I don't know if I was already saved as a child walking down the church aisle years ago, but I do know that day, as a college senior who'd made an absolute mess of life, I was a new person. I knew I'd never be the same. I didn't want to spend one day of my life without Jesus, and I told Him I'd go anywhere He wanted me to. And I have.

And you can too. So if you haven't accepted Jesus yet, stop right now. Surrender to Jesus wherever you are. You don't have to live with fear, shame, or regret anymore. There's absolutely nothing you can do or have done that makes you unworthy of Him. You don't need a church and you don't need a preacher. God is right where we are, and He meets us right where we are. And all those mistakes brought you right here, right now. So, embrace them and forgive yourself. I don't regret my mistakes because they brought me to Jesus. There's nothing He can't make right.

xoxo

Introducing Him

Amen! Amen! Oh, sorry, I was amening my wife. Hi, I'm Sam, and that's my wife Tonya. Great to meet y'all! You can probably tell by the long, drawn-out accent that, yes, I am from the South. In fact, I would love to share my story with you. So, pour yourself a glass of iced tea, kick your feet up, and enjoy some Southern hospitality.

I don't remember, but mom says that as a boy I wanted to talk to our pastor. Apparently, I didn't want to talk about joining the church, being baptized, or getting saved; rather, I wanted to learn how to become a pastor. How I would love to hear that conversation today! Soon after that conversation, Dad's job transferred our family to Longview, TX. We didn't know it then, but our lives would never be the same.

Highway 49, which weaves its way through the state of Mississippi, is one of the deadliest highways in America. We learned firsthand just how deadly. It was the summer of 1984, and we were in the process of moving. Dad was driving the van. I was in the passenger seat, which was a huge deal for a ten-year-old, and Mom was lying on the folded down seat in the back. She was not feeling well due to being pregnant—unaware. My six-year old brother, Joey, was sitting in the second row of seats. I vividly remember driving through the drive-thru at McDonalds on Highway 49 in Richland, MS. Dad was sleepy and needed some caffeine. When I was an adult, Mammaw said that I once told her that dad kept dozing off while driving on that dreadful day.

After we stopped at McDonald's, all went dark. I just can't recall any other memories of that tragic day. Our van hit the back of that eighteen-wheeler with such force that dad died upon impact. He must have fallen asleep. Joey was rushed to the hospital by the first highway patrolman on site. The jaws of life cut me out of the van and under the dashboard. Mom spent the most time in the hospital. We all survived except dad. Even my unborn sister, Angel, survived. In a short span of time, Mom learned that Dad was dead and that she was pregnant. God took Dad but gave us Angel.

From that day forward, Highway 49 represented death for our family. But God. Though we didn't meet until many years later, my wife Tonya grew up in Richland, MS, right off of Highway 49. She lived about one mile from that very McDonald's where we stopped in 1984 before the wreck. When Tonya and I got married, we bought a house in Richland, right off of Highway 49. We joined First Baptist Church Richland that is on Highway 49. God called me to pastor out of that same church on Highway 49. God transformed Highway 49 from a highway of death to a highway of life. God gave me Tonya, a church family, a home, and a vocational calling to pastor. He did it all at the very place where He took Dad. But God!

I am getting ahead of myself. Let's go back to where it all started, Crystal Springs, MS, or, as most of the people from obscure, tiny towns in South, Mississippi say, "I grew up about half an hour from Jackson." Growing up a Greer meant eating fried catfish. We had fish fries for birthdays, anniversaries, Christmas, Thanksgiving—you name it! Give the Greers a reason to gather, and on the menu will be a fish platter! Pulling up to Pawpaw's house and seeing a row of catfish bleeding out and hanging from cypress trees was normal. It's been said more than once, "Not all catfish eaters are Greers, but all Greers are catfish eaters." That is, until I came along. Sorry fam. I know. I ruined it. You see, I am allergic to fish. Don't feel too sorry for me because each time the fish fryer was fired up Mammaw cooked me a steak. Yummy!

Growing up a Greer also meant going to church. No, I don't mean darkening the doors every other Sunday. We found reasons to be at church every day. In fact, the Greers didn't find excuses to miss church. Church was the excuse to miss everything else. A shout out to my mom for always making sure we didn't miss church. Thanks, Mom! Even the businesses in Crystal Springs closed on Wednesdays at noon, so the town could get ready to go to church. Townspeople piled into the Methodist, Presbyterian, and Baptist church every Wednesday night. Sundays? Sundays? Forget about finding any business open on Sundays. Of course, this was the late 1980s and early 1990s.

I don't remember hearing it. If I did, I probably wasn't listening. You know, the gospel. From the age of ten to eighteen, hearing sermons preached at the United Methodist Church was on our family's Sunday itinerary. I thought I was as faithful of a Christian as they come.

Yes, I had it all in check. Sprinkled as an infant? Check. Completed confirmation class at twelve years old? Check. Joined the church? Check. Attended the church? Check. Served as an acolyte? Check. Not drinking alcohol? Check. Not doing drugs? Check. Befriended everyone? Check. Saying the right things at the right time? Check. Trying harder? Check. Being nicer? Check. Doing more good than bad (or so I thought)? Check. Under the religious façade, I was nothing more than an empty shell. No peace. No joy. No hope. No satisfaction.

Aunt Trudy and Uncle Devon were relentless. Not only did they invite me to Harmony Baptist Church, they never stopped knocking until I opened that door. You heard right! Asking wasn't enough for them. Praying for me to come wasn't enough for them. They came knocking on the door of that apartment until I opened it. Man, am I glad I did! I guess they took Jesus at His Word when He said in Matthew 5:7:

Ask, and it will be given to you; seek, and you will find, knock, and it will be opened to you.

Jesus is teaching His disciples to humbly request by asking, to humbly request and add a bit of action by seeking, and to humbly request and never stop knocking. Did I mention that Aunt Trudy and Uncle Devon were relentless as they never stopped knocking?

Pastor Clark Stewart opened the Bible and preached the gospel. He preached about the sacrificial death, burial, and resurrection of Jesus. I can't remember his sermon title or text, but the Holy Spirit revealed the following: (1) God loves Sam, (2) Sam has sinned against God, (3) God gave Jesus to rescue Sam from himself and his sin, (4) Jesus willingly died on the cross instead of Sam, (5) Jesus was buried on behalf of Sam, (6) Jesus was raised to life to give Sam life, and (7) Sam can confess with his mouth that Jesus is Lord and believe in his heart that God raised Jesus from the dead to be saved.

Well, was I gloriously saved on that Sunday? No. Was I under heavy conviction to move toward God and be saved? Yes. What happened? Hold you horses. I am getting to it. I went home that day without making a decision for Jesus. Thankfully, the Holy Spirit didn't let up. The next morning, I called Aunt Trudy and told her something was wrong. I was feeling something strange. She knew exactly what was going on. She called one of the pastors, and we met at her house. He walked through some selected Scriptures in Romans known as the Roman Road. I heard the gospel again, but this time I responded. At the age of twenty-one, I knelt at Aunt Trudy's couch, and I asked Jesus to save me. You could say that I was saved on the Roman Road with my Aunt standing by. Now, peace!   Now, joy! Now, hope! Now, satisfaction is mine!

Y'all, Jesus not only gave me victory, but He gave me a new vocation! It took me a while to answer His call, but answer I did. Two years into marriage, Tonya and I went on our first mission trip to Myanmar. Part of our mission involved dropping Burmese translated Bibles out of the window of a train that traveled across the Burmese countryside. We were ready for this challenge. But there was a threefold problem: (1) the train was delayed for twelve hours, (2) Burmese Bibles were illegal, and (3) two armed Burmese soldiers on our train car were watching us like hawks. After a few hours, the soldiers fell asleep and we were able to drop all the Bibles.

Upon arriving at our destination, we were exhausted from the thirty-hour plus day, wet from the torrential downpour of rain, and hungry for food. Feeling sorry for myself, I fell back on the bed. God spoke. No, not audibly but louder than audibly. He brought to memory the prayer a missionary prayed for Tonya and me before we left. "Lord, please open the eyes of the people who need to see these Bibles being dropped and close the eyes of the people who don't." God impressed on my spirit:

> Sam, I purposely delayed that train so those soldiers would fall asleep and My Word could get to the people who need to hear. Sam, this is not about you. You choose this day whom you will serve. Me or you?!

Yes, I chose God, and I still do. I couldn't wait to tell Tonya that God was calling us to serve as missionaries in Myanmar. Tonya said, "I didn't hear that phone ring!" The first Sunday after we returned from Myanmar, God allowed me to preach in a new church plant. Immediately, it was clear that God was calling me to pastor a local church. Tonya and I said "Yes"!

Have you said "yes" to Jesus? Some of you have yet to say "yes" to being saved. You can right now. Jesus is calling. Ask Him to save you. Some of you have yet to answer "yes" to a call to ministry. Put this book down now. Right now. Answer Jesus. Say, "Yes"!

Introducing Him to Her

Before she said yes, how did Tonya and I meet? You might expect that Tonya and I met at church, right? Don't most pastors and their wives meet at church? Actually, the majority of the pastors who serve on our staff met their wives at church. Except for us. We met in a club. No, we didn't meet in a backyard Bible club, not a book club, not a country club, not even a fitness club, but, you know, a nightclub. We met on the dance floor. I was running from God's call on my life and Tonya had yet to surrender to the Lord. Yet, God brought us together.

After we started dating and before we got married, there was a popular song by Jagged Edge called "Let's Get Married". We had no idea that this song, which soon became "our song," would define us so well. Reverend Run-DMC raps verse three of this song, and the lyrics describe our story most accurately. Listen to this:

> What's going on across the seas?

> It ain't nothin; I ain't frontin'
> Shorty comin' with me
> Now I done already gave you the key to the Range
> And your last name 'bout to change
> Now you Mrs. Simmons, gotta betta livin'
> What a difference Rev-Run made
> Used to be the snake type, hangin' out late night
> Girl, you done made me change my life
> Ever since you met me, keys to the Bentley
> Now they call you the preacher's wife
> I'm the type of guy that take you out
> And buy that ring with the rock that'll break your arm
> Playas won't try that, now you can't deny that
> Triple, dub, Rev to the Run dot comi

The highlighted verses above capture our story. When we decided this would be "our song," we had no idea that one day Tonya would be a preacher's wife and that I would be that preacher. Me a preacher? Are you kidding me? No way! You joking, right? You see, I was the snake type hanging out all hours of the night. But God used Tonya to change my life by getting my attention back on Him. The only highlighted part of that verse that isn't accurate is that we've been married twenty years and Tonya still doesn't have the keys to the Bentley, nor do I.

Now that we have introduced ourselves, we would love for you to continue to join us for more conversations. Why another book on marriage? Tonya and I are tired of seeing marriage mocked. We are sick and tired of seeing marriages and families destroyed by the flesh, the world, and Satan. We are passionate about helping couples engage one another in everyday life. Our culture is suffering from the symptoms of the abandonment of biblical marriage. As a result, our nation is wasting time trying to eliminate symptoms while sinking further into the sin of discounting biblical marriage. We believe that marriage is the perfect place for imperfect people to be perfected.

While applying for the ISBN number for this book, we were reminded of just how much marriage is dismissed. One step in securing an ISBN number for a book is to choose a genre. No, not gender, but genre. The list of genres on the ISBN website is impressive with genres such as: astrology, cooking, crime, education, games, gardening, health, interior-decorating, self-help, parenting, pets, travel, wit and humor, just to name a few. You might guess that the genre of a book on marriage would be marriage, right? Wrong. Of all the genres listed on the ISBN website, marriage was not even on the list. That is the very reason why we are writing a book on biblical marriage.

Our hope in writing this book is to cause a super-spreader experience. That is, we hope this book sparks a super spread of gospel conversational marriages. We hope to accomplish this via ten conversations laid out in this book. Our prayer is that whether you are newly married, nearly married, numbly married (going through the motions), or narrowly married (separated), you and your spouse will experience a gospel conversational marriage. Also, we pray that all marrieds, remarrieds, unmarrieds, one-day-hope-to-be-marrieds, never-wanna-get-marrieds, or wish-we-weren't-marrieds, would find satisfaction, healing, and hope in the gospel of Jesus.

What is a gospel conversational marriage? A gospel conversational marriage is a marriage whereby a husband and wife experience God in their marriage. If you want to have a gospel conversational marriage and experience God in your marriage, then you must marry the gospel to your marriage. Tonya and I are committed to having a gospel conversational marriage by experiencing God in our marriage one conversation at a time. How about you? Join the conversation now!

Conversation 1

Marriage Made by Heaven

Therefore a man shall leave his father and mother and hold fast to his wife, and they shall become one flesh.
Genesis 2:24

What is your picture of marriage? Is a picture-perfect marriage possible? If so, how can I have a picture-perfect marriage?

Maui'd in Hawaii

Tonya and I were Maui'd in Hawaii. On May 21, 2001, we were married on the beach in Maui, Hawaii. We were blessed to have twenty of our family and friends join us. You guessed it. Convincing them to come to our wedding wasn't too difficult. My Uncle Jim even says to this day, "Sam, y'all's was the best wedding ever." We know, right? For crying out loud, it was a wedding made in the earthly paradise—Hawaii!

Ten years later, on May 21, 2011, Harold Camping predicted the world would end. Tonya and I were humbled to think that Mr. Camping would select our wedding anniversary for his end times prediction. What a fantastic storyline! Tonya and I were married in the earthly paradise, Hawaii, and on our ten-year anniversary we would be ushered into the heavenly paradise, Heaven. As you know, the world didn't end on May 21, 2011. Yep, hard to believe. Let's get back to our wedding day.

Boys will be boys. The groomsmen and I arrived at the beach before Tonya and her bridesmaids. So, we did what any immature twenty-somethings would do on the beach in Maui. We jumped in the water. Yes, before the ceremony. Give us a little credit as we did at least roll up the bottom part of our khakis just below our knees. OK! Ok, I admit. Jumping in the water before the ceremony was a bad choice. But having a destination wedding was a great choice.

One harp, eight in the wedding party, and a Christian ceremony made for an unforgettable destination wedding. Sadly, too many couples have an unforgettable destination wedding that ends in a forgettable marriage. Forget about it. Marriage should never be forgotten or forgettable.

Think about it. Seriously. Of all the things that God made prior to the Fall, marriage is the only one of the four institutions (marriage, family, church, government) that God instituted before sin crashed the party. Most of the accounts in the Bible occurred after the Fall, but what happened before the Fall?

What Happened Before the Fall?

Creation

Out of nowhere, she is now here. No heads up. No warning. Tonya's coming in strong. Both of her hands rubbing some cold, potent, slightly burning substance on my face. Essential oils. 'Nuff said. Where's my fellow essential oil husbands at? Several years ago, when Tonya first started researching essential oils, I told her the only essential oil is whatever oil is used to cook those Chick-fil-A waffle fries! That is an essential oil. Now, a few years later, I love essential oils. I use them more than Tonya. It is biblical! Essential oils are a part of God's creation before the Fall. In Revelation 22:1-2, the Bible says:

Then the angel showed me the river of the water of life, bright as crystal, flowing from the throne of God and of the Lamb, through the middle of the street of the city; also, on either side of the river, the tree of life with its twelve kinds of fruit, yielding its fruit each month. The leaves of the tree were for the healing of the nations.

Essential oils are produced from the leaves and roots of trees and plants. The Tree of Life in Revelation is the same tree of life in the Garden of Eden which means the same leaves of healing found in Revelation were created in Genesis.

Arguably, the five most important words in the Bible are the first five found in Genesis 1:1:

In the beginning, God created...

Our Creator God created all of creation. Creation was certainly created before the Fall. Nothing in all creation was made apart from the Creator. *In the beginning* leaves no room for debate. All of creation starts with our Creator God. *God created* leaves no room for debate over the existence of God. The purpose of the Bible is not for you to merely know God exists; rather, it is for you to know God and make Him known. Marriage is one of the best platforms to know God and to make Him known.

What Happened Before the Fall?

Creativity

Have you looked up from your screen long enough to be reminded of God's creativity in creation? One of my favorite activities as a child was cloud watching. No, not Google Cloud, iCloud or The Cloud. Cloud watching. I can remember looking up in the sky and naming which animal I saw in the cloud. Of the hundreds of times I played that game, I never remember saying, "God, we have already seen that cloud." No two clouds I have ever seen have been the same. Why? God's creativity is on full display in the clouds.

Think of all the creatures God has made. Many of which have never been seen as they lie deep on the ocean floor. God is so creative that He creatively allowed Adam to get in on His creativity by allowing him to name all the animals. In Genesis 2:19, the Bible says:

Now out of the ground the LORD God had formed every beast of the field and every bird of the heavens and brought them to the man to see what he would call them. And whatever the man called every living creature, that was its name.

How fun that must have been. Adam did a fairly good job. Think about how funny and strange it would be to call a *horse* anything other than a *horse*. Come to think of it, I can think of a more appropriate name for our dog, Bailey—*The Devil Wears Fur*. Y'all, that dog barks at me every day when I come home and has for three years. No, I am not bitter. Maybe a little. Back to Adam.

God gave Adam dominion over every living thing. Of course, this was before the Fall. Now, after the Fall, all of creation is tainted with sin and its symptoms. If you don't believe in the Fall, just get a cat. No human beings, including Adam and Eve, have ever had any dominion over a feline. Nonetheless, God intends you to be creative in your marriage. Don't waste all your creativity at work, school, church, and other activities. Save the best creativity for your marriage.

What Happened Before the Fall?

Gender

Tonya's bestie recently went to her doctor for an annual check-up. She was asked to fill out some paperwork and that is where she noticed it. She had never seen such a question before. Odd. Strange. Certainly, it was surprising to say the least, especially in the office of a doctor who sees female patients exclusively. She was asked to write her name and then the next blank asked for her *preferred pronouns.* Preferred pronouns? Huh? She wrote in the blank, "I'm not sure what this means." Obvious questions arise: (1) why are members of the female gender being asked their gender, and (2) why is the word *pronouns* plural? Isn't the paperwork filled out by one patient at a time?

The genesis of gender is found in the book of Genesis. I have recently read there are now upwards of sixty-four genders and identity expression terms.[ii] Heartbreaking to think of the number of people who are confused about their identity. God's original design for the sexes is two—male and female. In Genesis 1:27, we read:

So God created man in his own image, in the image of God he created him; male and female he created them.

More questions. Is this text teaching that God is both genders? If so, shouldn't people be free to identify with whichever gender they choose? Does this Scripture mean that God is *androgynous*, that is, partly male and partly female simultaneously? If God is both male and female, then shouldn't human beings made in God's image have the liberty of being either male or female based on personal preference? A doctor's office inquiry of *preferred pronouns* makes more sense if human beings have the authority to choose. So, do we?

Responsible Bible students will pay attention to pronouns. Two pronouns in Genesis 1:27 bring clarity to this conversation. Each time I hear this verse read aloud, two words parachute out of this passage as they seem to be at odds with one another—*him* and *them*. *Him* is singular: in the image of God he created *him*. *Them* is plural: male and female he created *them*. What is going on?

Gender is not about our preferences; it is about God's providence. *In the beginning, God,* reminds us that our starting point must be God, not self. The *him* in Genesis 1:27 refers to the whole of mankind, that is, the human race. The *them* in Genesis 1:27 refers to the two groups by which God has divided up the human race, male and female. The beauty of marriage in relation to gender is that the image of God is most fully revealed in the human race when a man and a woman are united in marriage.

Fight for your marriage. Why? When you fight for *your* marriage you are fighting for marriage. By the way, *your* marriage is worth the fight because marriage is worth the fight. Why? Remember, the image of God is most fully revealed in the union of a man and a woman in marriage.

What Happened Before the Fall?

Sleep

Are you a nap taker? One of the huge differences Tonya and I had to work through in marriage was the taking of naps. Tonya grew up taking naps. I grew up never taking naps because of two primary reasons. First, my mother grew up as a pastor's kid. She and my grandmother would accompany my grandfather as he preached at three different churches on Sundays. When he was finished, the whole family went home to take naps. Every Sunday of my mom's childhood was spent taking naps. To this day, my mother loathes taking naps. Second, after my dad died, my mother never wanted to be at home. We were always on the go. We went to the movies. We went to the mall. We went to the bowling alley. We went to the park. Go. Go. Go. So, when Tonya and I were married we had different expectations. On Saturday and Sunday afternoons, Tonya expected us to take a nap, while I expected us to be on the go.

Over the past twenty years of marriage, I have learned that one of the best spiritual disciplines one can practice is sleeping. I like pillows. I like big pillows. I like fluffy pillows. I like the cool side of big, fluffy pillows. Without question, the best pillow to lay one's head on is the pillow of the sovereignty of God. You see, the sovereignty of God is what makes sleep a spiritual discipline along the road to spiritual maturity. When a believer sleeps, he or she is trusting in the sovereignty of God. The psalmist wrote in Psalm 127:2:

It is in vain that you rise up early and go late to rest, eating the bread of anxious toil; for he gives to his beloved sleep.

God not only gives His beloved sleep, but He gives *to* His beloved *in* their sleep. God answers so many prayers while we sleep. God never stops working even while we are sleeping. One of the most vivid examples of God giving to his beloved *in* their sleep is that found when God caused Adam to go into a deep sleep. In Genesis 2:21, the Bible says:

So the LORD God caused a deep sleep to fall upon the man, and while he slept took one of his ribs and closed up its place with flesh. And the rib that the LORD God had taken from the man he made into a woman and brought her to the man. Then the man said, "This at last is bone of my bones and flesh of my flesh; she shall be called Woman, because she was taken out of Man."

Adam named every living creature that paraded by, but none was found suitable for him. Can you imagine what Adam must have thought when he woke up? Do you remember the first time you saw your spouse? What did you say? If not married, what do you think you will say the first time you see your future spouse? Adam said, *at last*! Preach! What a word!

Literally, Eve was the only woman on earth for Adam and vice versa. God made Eve for Adam. Husbands, God made your bride just for you. Wives, God made your hubs just for you. Of all the spouses on planet earth, God made yours just for you. What's more, there is no other spouse on earth for you other than yours.

Wow! Did you hear that? Sounds like a marriage not made by Hollywood, but a marriage made by Heaven. What is a marriage made by Heaven?

What Is a Marriage *by* Heaven?

It seemed like a good idea at the time. What, getting married? Oh, getting married wasn't a good idea, it was a great idea! Just ask my bride, Tonya. So, what seemed like a good idea at the time? Early on in a new pastorate, it seemed like a good idea to celebrate all the couples in the church married fifty years or more. Seating all of them in the front, middle section of the worship center seemed like the thing to do. But what happens when what seems like the thing to do comes undone at the seams?

It played out like so. On that fateful Sunday morning, the seats were reserved, the couples were beaming with excitement, the roses were ready to be given to each bride, the order of service was set, but something seemed off. Gathering all the long-lasting lovebirds in the center section nearly emptied the room. Instead of spreading out in their usual seats, they were unusually packed in like sardines. As I looked out over the congregation, I was surprised not by what I saw but what I didn't see.

Where were the children and the grandchildren of these couples? Where were the younger marrieds and the not so younger marrieds? I couldn't help but think, "Could this be the last generation of couples who would make it to the Golden Anniversary and beyond?" Were these couples the last of the once unmarrieds to actually get married and stay married? Was marriage disappearing before our very eyes? Wait, we need to focus. Mulling over questions like these should never be part of a celebration of marriage, right? Wow, what a sobering moment!

GOSPEL CONVERSATIONAL MARRIAGE

One of the glaring takeaways from that Sunday morning celebration of marriage was the missing marrieds. All of the marrieds in the room that morning either had no hair or gray hair. Younger marrieds were missing. What a stark reminder that marriage is in the crosshairs and Satan has his finger on the trigger. What has happened to marriages made by Heaven? Sure, marriage is work, but it works. God's design for marriage ensures that marriage works. Before the Fall, God revealed His plan for marriages that work. In Genesis 2:24, the Bible says:

Therefore a man shall leave his father and his mother and hold fast to his wife, and they shall become one flesh.

Come in here real close! Don't miss this! The biblical concept of *leaving and cleaving* is on full display. *Leaving and cleaving* is the reality of a man and a woman leaving their parents and cleaving to one another in marriage. What does that look like? What does it mean to leave? Three important ways couples must leave: (1) physically, (2) financially, & (3) emotionally.

Physically. Men and women, there comes a time when it is time to move out of mom and dad's house. At some point, we must leave mom and dad physically, that is, we must get out from under their roof. Some couples get married and never move away from mom and dad. Geographically, that is ok. Moving out from under your parents' roof is essential, but relocating to a different town or neighborhood isn't always necessary. God's design for marriage is for the husband and wife to be on their own. The hardest thing that Tonya and I have ever done was the best thing we could have ever done. We moved away. We moved to a different state. We have yet to go back.

Financially. Oof! Ouch! Watch the toes! This one hits close to home. So close. Not only does this one get on our front porch, it marches into our kitchen. Tonya and I have done a better job leaving physically than we have financially. Leaving financially doesn't mean that parents are unable to help their married children from time to time.

What it certainly means is that the married children are not to be on mom and dad's payroll. Mom and dad shouldn't be paying their married children's bills month to month. Work toward leaving mom and dad financially.

Emotionally. Well, now you've done it! This one, right? This one is the toughest by far. I have personally counseled too many couples who have left mom and dad physically and financially but not emotionally. Most often, this is how it goes. The husband and wife have an argument that turns into a fight. Rather than sticking it out and talking through it, one or both spouses run off to mom or dad. What a dangerous way to get stuck! If you want to get unstuck in your marriage, then you have to stick together when you get stuck. Stick it out! Don't stick it out just for your kids' sake, but stick it out for your sake!

Tonya and I have stuck it out for twenty years. It hasn't always been easy, but it has always been worth it. Listen as she tells you our story about leaving and cleaving. Oh no, Tonya really didn't like that leaving part too much. Yeah, she didn't like it at all. She tells it better than I ever could. Listen up!

She Says

Ladies, I wanted to take a moment to talk about that leaving and cleaving stuff. Us girls tend to cleave to our mommas, so this gets on my toes big time. I told you earlier that my parents were divorced and that I spent a lot of time without my momma. I also watched her live through 12 years in an abusive marriage (not my dad). To say I longed for my mom's attention is an understatement. Abusive marriages are all consuming, so getting her attention away from that was not an easy feat. My mom was only a few years out of that marriage before I found myself getting married. I'd moved off to college recently, but every time I got the chance, I hopped in my little red sports car and zoomed home to momma. She had Thursday afternoons off and we loved to spend them shopping. So, I often skipped my 8am classes on Fridays.

Matter of fact, when Sam proposed my junior year of college, I had a hard time nailing down a wedding date. Thank goodness daddy said he wouldn't give his blessing until I graduated college. So that gave me two years! But in no time graduation rolled around and Sam was putting the pressure on to nail down a date. I remember him sitting me down at momma's kitchen table one weekend with a calendar. I couldn't avoid it any longer. This man was gonna get me out of my momma's house and I'd just gotten her back!

The next few months went by in a daze. I finished college and had five months to plan a wedding. My wonderful in-laws gifted us with a honeymoon to Hawaii, and since I'd figured out that planning weddings just wasn't my thing, we decided to get Maui'd! It was spectacular! Other than all the fellas being soaking wet when I arrived at the venue. The pictures will be an eternal reminder of the maturity level of the man I married.

I'll never forget after the wedding. It truly hit me that I wasn't going home to my momma-a-nem, as we say in Mississippi. Instead of being overjoyed like most brides, I CRIED on my wedding night! Sam was so sweet and promised me I could go see my momma in the hotel next door in the morning.

Y'all. If that ain't the opposite of "leaving and cleaving" I don't know what is. My momma was on my honeymoon!! So I spent my first day of wedded bliss going to see my momma!

Sam and I had already bought a house within a few miles of both my parents so the transition wasn't too bad—at least for the first couple of years. Isn't God so gracious? He gave me two and a half years to adjust to this leaving and cleaving stuff before the real test came. My man would soon move me OUT OF THE STATE!

We'd joined this church not far from our new little house and, y'all, this preacher! He must have thought I was NUTS! The whole congregation probably thought so too because I just cried through his whole sermon. He spoke to me alone week after week! So many things I didn't know! I was a brand-new believer, brand new wife, brand new college grad, brand new employee and brand-new homeowner all at the same time. I'd just started figuring out who I was when EVERYTHING changed. I needed so much direction and Brother Chuck gave it to me every single Sunday. If that man said go on a mission trip to Burma, we went. If he said show up Saturday morning to go follow up with VBS kids, we were there! If he said to take over a Sunday school class, we were in!

But then it happened. He called Sam and scheduled a time to come see us at our house. Y'all. I scrubbed the house from top to bottom. I had fresh flowers. I made snacks. I fixed my hair and make-up—I don't often do that on Saturdays, because I worked hard all week and liked my Saturday naps!

But he wasn't interested in any of that. He didn't eat my snacks or even visit the bathroom to see how clean my toilets were. All I remember is this humble, kind, godly man on his knees in front of us wanting to hear our testimony and know how we came to meet Jesus. After we told him what we just told you, he started talking about seminary and how New Orleans Baptist Theological Seminary would be the best school. I didn't have any idea what seminary was, but it was obvious Sam did. Sam even told him he'd felt the call for years and had been avoiding it. Huh? What was he talking about and why was I finding this out AFTER he rushed me down the aisle? Bait and switch I tell ya! I was too embarrassed to ask what seminary was in front of Brother Chuck but as soon as he left, I demanded Sam tell me. Oh, HUH-UH! No way was I moving that far away from my mom and dad.

Six months later we had quit our jobs, put our house up for sale, and moved two and a half hours away to New Orleans, Louisiana.

I'd resisted leaving and cleaving as long as I could. I even kept my job in Mississippi and stayed behind a few weeks because I didn't have a job in New Orleans yet and our house hadn't sold. How would we pay the bills? I had to keep working. It wasn't long before I knew that wasn't the right thing to do. My man was trying to lead, and all I could hear God say was, "Trust your husband." Let me be clear when I say I never felt a call to full time ministry. Never. Ever. But Sam did, and we were at a place where I had to trust and obey. Leave and cleave. And so, we did.

Some of my bridesmaids showed up to the wedding in a jeep with the top off. It sporadically rains in Hawaii, and you guessed it, they were wet for the ceremony too. If I could rewind time 20 years, I would not have let that bother me one bit. Thankfully I didn't spend too much energy being mad when I saw all the smiles on everyone else's faces.

Things just work out when you are following God's calling. When He tells you what to do, just do it. That takes a lot of discipline because our wants and desires get in the way and hearing Him can often seem muddy. He always wants what's best for us. Always. Don't fear it. If what's best for your marriage is leaving your parents, do it. I promise you will never regret following God's command. His ways are so much better. I still love my mom and dad and love being with them, but I'm so glad we answered God's call. The riches He's blessed us with since then have endlessly enriched our lives. There's not one need we've ever had in which He hasn't provided. Even in the tough times, I could see Him everywhere.

They told us in Hawaii that rain on your wedding day was a good sign. "No rain, no rainbows" has been the story of our lives. Struggling through the hard things together has brought us the most beautiful treasures. I can't wait to tell you more!

xoxo

Great word, Boo Boo! Well, all except the maturity level of the man you married comment. And the "bait and switch" to get you to marry me comment. Oh, by the way, my nickname for Tonya is Boo Boo. What Pastor Fred Luter calls his wife, I could also apply to Tonya: "The love of my life, the apple of my eye, my prime rib, my good thing!" So, what does it look like to cleave? Well, we started with *leave* because you can't *cleave* unless you *leave*. The word cleave means to "hold fast," "pursue," "be joined together."[iii] Wives, you and your hubs are a team. Husbands, you and your wife are a team. More than that, God says you are one flesh. God's design for marriage was not only made by heaven, but it was made in heaven.

What Is a Marriage Made *in* Heaven

Have you ever seen one? If so, you would know it. A picture-perfect marriage is hard to miss. Has one ever been seen on TV or any streaming service? Did Lucy and Ricky a generation ago have a picture-perfect marriage? Of course, I am asking for a *friend*, but what about Monica and Chandler? Aha, I know, the longest running union of Homer and Marge. Yeah, probably not—it is a cartoon. How about Bel-Air's Phil and Vivian? Perhaps it has been seen in the office with Jim and Pam. Or, maybe we see the vision of it in the marriage of Wanda and Vision.

What is a picture-perfect marriage? No, we probably shouldn't look to the *Bachelor* or *Bachelorette*. I am talking about a marriage even more perfect than what people post on their social media platforms. I am talking about a marriage not made in Hollywood but made in Heaven.

Ladies, what would a marriage made in Heaven look like for you? How about fresh flowers and every kind of fresh food your heart desires all day every day? No, not from the local florist and health food store, but from your own garden. That's right! Your own garden that your man works and keeps up. A garden flush with all that looks good, smells good, feels good, sounds good, and tastes good. By the way, all of the food and flowers would be in season all the time. Yes, endless cotton candy grapes! In Genesis 2:8-9, the
Bible says:

And the LORD God planted a garden in Eden, in the east, and there he put the man whom he had formed. And out of the ground the LORD

GOSPEL CONVERSATIONAL MARRIAGE

God made to spring up every tree that is pleasant to the sight and good for food.

And all the ladies said, "Amen to my man working that garden!" I know all the men are thinking, "What about us?" I haven't forgotten about us guys. Gentlemen, what would a marriage made in Heaven look like for you? How about you and your bride being naked all day every day? Sign me up! But wait, there's more. In addition to being naked with your bride, how about consuming all the food you could ever imagine and never gaining one pound? In Genesis 2:25, the Bible says:

And the man and his wife were both naked and were not ashamed.

Just think about never being ashamed of being naked because both man and wife are in peak physical condition. It just doesn't get any better than being naked with your spouse and unashamed. Again, sign me up now!

Hey y'all, these are great reasons why the very first marriage, the union of Adam and Eve, started out as the picture-perfect marriage. However, the best reason is that God joined Adam and Eve as they walked through the garden during the day. In Genesis 3:8-9, the Bible says:

And they heard the sound of the LORD God walking in the garden in the cool of the day, and the man and his wife hid themselves from the presence of the LORD God among the trees of the garden. But the LORD God called to the man and said to him, "Where are you?"

So. Many. Questions. Why are Adam and Eve hiding? How did they know to hide? Why is God asking their whereabouts? Yes, this is after Adam and Eve sinned against God by ignoring and disobeying Him. Yes, God knew their exact local. God is the original GPS. Watch this! God asking the whereabouts of Adam and Eve suggests that He would often spend time with them in the garden. C'mon, the first day that God decided to go hang out with Adam and Eve wouldn't be on the day of the inaugural sin. Obviously, it was God's daily practice to kick it with Adam and Eve.

Wait. What? Wow! God Himself hung out with the first married couple. God Himself was included in the first marriage. Get this! God wants to be included in your marriage. He wants to bless your marriage. He wants to hang out with you and your spouse. God wants to be the host of not only your wedding but your marriage. Somebody hold my diet root beer with vanilla for a bit while I have a Holy Spirit fit! What made the very first marriage a marriage made in Heaven was not Adam or Eve, but God.

A picture-perfect marriage is one that brings God into the picture. Invite Jesus into your marriage. A little boy was telling his parents about the story of the wedding at Cana he had heard in Sunday School. His parents asked, "What did you learn from the wedding at Cana?" He replied, "If you are going to have a wedding, make sure Jesus is there!" Cha Ching! Yes! Invite Jesus not only to your wedding but into your marriage!

God's design for marriage is not that we ask more of our spouse than we ask of God. Quite the opposite. Ask more of God and less of your spouse. Talk to God before talking to your spouse. Sometimes we have to ask God to help us care about something as much as our spouse cares. We should ask God to help us think of something to thank our spouse for each day. These are examples of bringing God into the picture. I know Coach Nick Saban often says, "Stop asking!" But God says, "Don't ever stop asking!" Ask God to help you affirm, encourage, and build-up your spouse. Have a conversation with God about having conversations with your spouse.

CONVERSATION STARTERS

1. Read Genesis 1 and 2. Pray and thank God for prioritizing marriage. How can you better prioritize your marriage? If single, how can you prioritize marriage?

2. In what ways should your marriage be impacted by the fact God made your spouse in His image?

3. Make a list of ways you can be creative in your marriage. Compare with one another.

4. Do you struggle more with leaving your parents physically, financially, or emotionally? Explain and discuss.

Conversation 2

Marriage, What A God Idea

Then the LORD God said, "It is not good that the man should be alone; I will make him a helper fit for him."
Genesis 2:18

Whose idea was marriage? Is marriage a good idea? Is marriage necessary? Is marriage outdated? Does marriage need a makeover?

What a God Idea

All marriages come to an end. Sure, that is not a great way to start a conversation about marriage. Or, is it? Did it grab your attention? If so, goal accomplished! Think about it. Sadly, some marriages do end in divorce. But even marriages that last a lifetime on earth, end in death. What's more, most wedding ceremonies include the bride and groom committing "till death do us part." Though, for us guys, we are only really listening for the phrase "You may kiss your bride." Of course, right? I know I was. Whether by divorce or death, all marriages come to an end. The question for this conversation is from where or from whom do marriages begin.

Biblical marriage continues to be under assault in America. With a desire to be inclusive, LGBTQ uses a plus sign (+) not a minus sign (-). Hence, LGBTQ+ is not LGBTQ-. But what happens when advocates for consensual incest, supporters of polygamy, or lobbyists for pedophilia want to be decriminalized and be included in true marriage equality? Through the lens of the world, these groups have every right to pursue what they think is true marriage equality. Through the lens of the Word, one man and one woman joined together is what God has coined as marriage.

You understand that first and foremost marriage is not a government idea, not a Google idea, not a global idea, not this group's idea, not that group's idea, not merely a good idea, not merely a great idea; marriage is God's idea. God created it. God designed it. God defined it. God continues to affirm it and bless it. How can we be sure that God created marriage and continues to affirm it and bless it?

God the Father Affirms Marriage. The Greek word for "marriage" refers to the state of being married. From the beginning of Scripture to the end, marriage is only and always between a man and a woman. Let's begin at the beginning. In Genesis 2:18, God said:

It is not good that the man should be alone; I will make a helper fit for him.

Church, that's good! Before the Fall, the only thing in all of creation that was NOT good was man being alone. How good is God? God is so good that He refused to leave man alone! I am so glad God refused to leave me alone! Aren't you so glad God doesn't leave you alone? Praise break! Give God a SHOUT of praise! Thank you, Lord! Thank you!

To fulfill His promise, God said HE would make a helper fit for Adam, and when God said it, He meant it, right? God was making a promise to not leave mankind alone. Think about it. Even for those who are single, widowed, divorced, not yet married, and never going to be married, God doesn't leave those alone either. In fact, God promised His disciples that He would send the *Helper*. Who is the Helper? The Helper is the Holy Spirit. Now that I have caught the rabbit that I was chasing, let's get back to the beginning. To fulfill His promise, in Genesis 2:20-22, the Bible says:

The man gave names to all livestock and to the birds of the heavens and to every beast of the field. But for Adam there was not found a helper fit for him. So the LORD God caused a deep sleep to fall upon the man, and while he slept took one of his ribs and closed up its place with flesh. And the rib that the LORD God had taken from the man he made into a woman and brought her to the man.

God made Eve from the rib of Adam. Where is the rib located? Which section of the body? Is it in the front of the body? Is it in the back of the body? No. Ribs are located on the side of the body. What a picture! God's design for marriage is for a husband and wife to walk together, side-by-side, as one flesh. One is not to be in front of the other or behind the other. The two are to walk in unison one with another. Matthew Henry said, "The woman was made of a rib out of the side of Adam; not made out of his head to top him, out of his feet to be trampled upon by him, but of his side to be equal with him, under his arm to be protected and near his heart to be beloved."[iv]

The first thing God did after He made Eve from the rib of Adam was to bring them together in a marriage relationship. Yeah, I guess God might have caused Adam to wake-up first. But then God brought Eve to Adam, and they were married. According to Genesis 2:24, it happened like so:

Therefore a man shall leave his father and mother and hold fast to his wife, and they shall become one flesh. And the man and his wife were both naked and were not ashamed.

God the Father has placed His stamp of approval on marriage as being between one man and one woman. The Bible never teaches that marriage is a necessity for every man and woman on earth; however, the Bible is clear that marriage is only and always between one man and one woman. Singleness is not a sin. Single-handedly redefining or redesigning marriage to fit one's lifestyle is an abomination. God the Father affirms marriage.

God the Son Affirms Marriage. Unpopular opinion: I don't like Jeopardy. I like Wheel of Fortune and Family Feud, but I don't like Jeopardy. Oh, I am sorry. "What is, I don't like Jeopardy?" Go ahead and judge me. I still don't like Jeopardy. Honestly, I am not smart enough to play the game. I would guess that Jesus loves Jeopardy. Why? Because you have to give your answer in the form of a question. Jesus often answered questions with a question. When asked about marriage in Matthew 19:3-6, Jesus answered with a question.

And Pharisees came up to him and tested him by asking, "Is it lawful to divorce one's wife for any cause?" He answered, "Have you not read that he who created them from the beginning made them male and female, and said, 'Therefore a man shall leave his father and mother and hold fast to his wife, and the two shall become one flesh'? So they are no longer two but one flesh. What therefore God has joined together, let not man separate."

Wow! Did you catch that? God the Son affirmed marriage in the exact same way as God the Father. Jesus didn't respond to the Pharisees' question by signing an executive order to redefine marriage. Jesus didn't entertain a marriage "Equality Act" for the purpose of being more inclusive of other lifestyles. Jesus didn't offer an alternative marriage relationship in addition to the marriage relationship between a man and a woman. Finally, Jesus didn't eliminate God's design due to divorce. Jesus affirmed the marriage relationship that was established in the Garden of Eden.

Did Jesus affirm marriage in other ways? Weddings (insert rolling eye emoji here). Oh, weddings. Don't get me wrong, though they consume a pastor's entire weekend, weddings are wonderful. But sometimes weddings can be, dare I say, overdone. When you fly-in the Chicago Boys Choir, ship lobster in from Maine, rent an entire Ruth's

GOSPEL CONVERSATIONAL MARRIAGE

Chris Steakhouse restaurant for the rehearsal dinner, rent out the Birmingham Convention Center, secure a police escort from the church to the convention center, rent a tugboat for the bride and groom to exit, and have a fireworks show that would rival Disney, you might have gone a wee bit too far. Or, it could be that one of your best friends from high school married the granddaughter of the owner of Cooper Tires.

On the other end of the spectrum is the simpler wedding like the one I officiated in the home of a lady whose family couldn't wait to party. Before the wedding, everyone was on their best behavior. The bridal party included the bride, the groom, and the pastor, that's me. Apparently, the start time of the wedding was only a suggestion. Most folks arrived thirty minutes late and no telling how long they were lit. Finally, family and friends gathered in the living room as I stood with the bride and groom at the fireplace. Short and sweet were the instructions from the bride. It was both short and sweet. After announcing the bride and groom as husband and wife, I mingled for a bit. I could tell that most everyone was quite antsy. Upon leaving, I realized why. As I walked out the door, I heard guests shouting, "The pastor's gone! Break out the liquor! Let's party!"

Jesus' first miracle was changing water to wine at a wedding. He not only affirmed marriage by what He said but also by what He did. Jesus cared enough about the marriage relationship between a man and a woman that He attended and hosted the wedding at Cana. God the Father and God the Son both affirm marriage.

God the Holy Spirit Affirms Marriage. All eyes were on Jordan. No one in the building and no one watching via TV believed anyone other than Jordan would take the potential game winning shot. Jordan drives the lane. His tongue hanging out. He pulls up. No! Wait! He dishes it out to Kerr. Just as soon as Kerr's hands touch the ball he shoots the jumper. SWISH! Bulls up by two with five seconds left! Scottie Pippen deflects Utah Jazz's inbound pass and the Bulls win! Bulls win! Steve Kerr, not Michael Jordan, hit the game winning shot to clinch the 1997 NBA Finals. What could be better than that?! How about meeting a young lady by the name of Tonya who told me she liked watching basketball and her favorite player was Steve Kerr?

What do you think happened next? Of course, our first year of dating was spent, in part, watching the Bulls win the 1998 NBA Finals. Little did I know Tonya was pulling one over on me! I was thrilled that I was dating a girl who loved sports as much as I did. Yeah, right! Think again. Since we have been married, she has never watched one game of any sport with me. No. Not. One. I love you Boo, Boo!

Watching the G.O.A.T (Greatest of All Time), Michael Jordan, is not what brought us together in marriage. Marriage is not the G.O.A.T.'s idea. Marriage is God's idea. God the Holy Spirit brought us together for the purpose of "going to the chapel and we're, gonna get married."[v] You see, along with God the Father and God the Son, God the Holy Spirit affirms marriage. In Ephesians 5:31, while teaching about marriage, the Holy Spirit led Paul to write:

Therefore a man shall leave his father and mother and hold fast to his wife, and the two shall become one flesh.

God the Holy Spirit didn't offer up alternatives to marriage outside the bond of one man and one woman. All three persons of the Trinity used the same definition to define marriage. Clearly, we must conclude that marriage is God's idea!

She Says

When Sam and I first started dating, he asked me one day, "Have you ever lived with anyone before?" Me and my youthful naivete had no idea what he meant. He clarified by telling me his mom wanted to know if I was the kinda girl that lived with boyfriends. The idea had never occurred to me, "NO! Have you??" I was glad to hear him say, "Do you know what my momma would do to me?" Whew. Ok, let's tackle the topic of cohabitating, shacking, living in sin, getting the milk for free, whatever you want to call it.

It wasn't long into my college and young adult years that I saw how common shacking was. Living with someone before you marry them. Trying things out. Tasting the milk before buying the cow. Seeing if this person is really someone you can live with before making the commitment. I've heard it all. I've heard of the tax breaks and government benefits you get for being unmarried. Isn't that just like the world? Making it easier to stay unmarried. Not valuing the covenant of marriage that God created. They define it every way we can imagine. I'm not sure if that's the overall goal or just us humans finding loopholes for getting around doing what's right. Either way, the Bible is very clear about keeping the marriage bed pure. Hebrews 13:4 says, "Let marriage be held in honor among all, and let the marriage bed be undefiled, for God will judge the sexually immoral and adulterous."

Ouch. God is very clear. This is just one of many passages where God calls for our purity. We aren't just following a rule when we obey, we are also avoiding all kinds of chaos. God is protecting us with His commands for us. It's for our own good. Think of all the troubles we avoid when we honor God with our actions.

Sam and I actually had some really good friends who were "living in sin" while we were in our newlywed days. The girl in the relationship *really* wanted to get married. The guy wanted a sample first. That became the center of their relationship, her chasing him and him finding ways to put her off. This had gone on for years already when we met them. Ladies, if a guy keeps telling you he's not sure, for the love, don't try to convince him. Do you really want to wonder for the rest of your life if he's only there because you talked him into it? And guys, if you aren't sure yet, she's probably not the girl for you and you should honor her enough to let her move on with her life and not drag her along waiting. She's worth more than that. And vice versa. This could go either way.

But I tell my girls all the time, "You teach people how to treat you." I wish I could take credit but that's really a Dr. Phil quote. Point is, if you don't value yourself enough to require more from a fella, chances are he won't value you either.

As a general rule, Sam requires an engaged couple he's counseling for marriage to have separate addresses. The Bible says in Genesis 2:24,

Therefore a man shall leave his father and mother and hold fast to his wife, and they shall become one flesh.

God calls us to come together in marriage. Not cohabitation.

I'm sad to say I don't know if our cohabitating friends made it. We were on two different paths in life and as we sought the Lord, He moved them from our lives. We tried but we weren't ready to coach them just yet. The last time we saw them was at a party at their house with a few other couples. Sam and I were stunned (and I was heartbroken) when we realized the reason they all kept taking turns slipping into the kitchen was to take shots without us. Ya know, since we were "good Christians."

If you are one of those couples who shacked first or are shacking now, Jesus is enough. He can cover it all. Yes, you are in disobedience of His word if you are currently living together without being married. But you can make it right. I know. You don't have the money to get separate places, and you depend on each other financially. I didn't say it would be easy. Following Jesus rarely is. But when He calls you to something, He will provide the way. So go pack up and wait for His instructions. Until then, go sleep on your best friend or parent's couch. Make this sacrifice that will honor God.

And He will forgive you. Don't live in that shame or regret. Use it as a teaching tool. Someone else will benefit from your story. That's why we all have a story; we can use it to encourage others.

xoxo

Marriage Needs a Takeover, Not a Makeover

What is the state of marriage in America? The American household is changing. Married couples leading the way in American households is no more. In 1949, 78.8% of all households contained married couples. Seventy-one years later, 48.2% of households contain married couples.[vi] In 2006, 49% of U.S. adults said it was "very important" for couples who have children together to be married. Only 29% say so in 2020.[vii] Yep, you guessed it! Cohabitation is on the rise. Thanks for that timely word on cohabitation, Boo Boo! It's now more common in America to have cohabited than to have married.[viii]

What is the state of marriage in the church in America? For nearly fifty years, people who attend church regularly marry at higher rates and divorce at lower rates than the rest of the population. Yes, you read that correctly! Christians who go to church on a regular basis are more likely to marry and less likely to divorce. How glad we should be to say and hear what we read in Psalm 122:1, "Let us go to the house of the LORD!" It seems that commitment to one's faith is strongly correlated with commitment to one's spouse, and there is no indication that this correlation will change anytime soon.[ix]

For those who are married, don't we all want more than just staying married and avoiding divorce? Don't we want an ongoing and ever-growing spiritual connection with our spouse? You see, for a man and a woman who are followers of Christ united in marriage, the question is not "How much of the Holy Spirit does our marriage have?" Rather, the question is, "How much of our marriage does the Holy Spirit have?" Yet, you and I both know that in Southern Baptist circles the Holy Spirit is treated like a left-handed, redheaded stepchild of the Trinity. Either we are scared of Him, ignore Him, forget about Him, or continually misunderstand Him. Where do we go from here?

SAM & TONYA GREER

Tonya and I Do Not Do Quiet Time Devotionals Together

I am about to confess something that is a "no-no" for a pastor and his wife. Here it goes! Tonya and I do not do quiet time devotionals together. Say it ain't so. Listen, you can hear a pin drop. Crickets. Before you throw this book in the trash, hear me out. When it comes to spiritual connectivity in marriage, God doesn't give us five ways to create spiritual unity. God gives us freedom. God doesn't give us a cookie-cutter model for spiritual unity in marriage. God gives us freedom. God doesn't give us a one-size-fits-all program for spiritual unity in marriage. God gives us freedom in regard to spiritual unity.

Tonya's idea of discipleship is so much better than mine. Mine is so mechanical. Hers is so free. Mine is so structured. Hers is so free. I have learned from Tonya the value of taking advantage of teachable moments and turning everyday conversations into gospel conversations. When it comes to daily devotionals, Tonya and I approach the Bible in opposite ways. Rather than forcing the other one to fit into a particular approach, we have chosen to have our personal quiet times alone with the Lord. Meanwhile, she and I have strong spiritual unity.

Let me give you some examples of our strong spiritual unity. Tonya and I have the same worldview (biblical) that affects the way we eat, where we go, what we watch, how we spend our money (most of the time), how we raise our girls, and how we relate to people, love people and serve people. For us, spiritual unity is a way of life. It's not just a lifestyle that is in style this season but out of style next season. No, spiritual unity is a way of life that affects ALL of our life. Biblical, spiritual unity is the lens by which we see the world. Spiritual unity is not relegated to one particular day on our calendar—being spiritually unified is our calendar. Spiritual unity doesn't happen at this time on this day—spiritual unity happens all the time, every day. We don't just talk about Jesus in a devotional time five times a week and then go live how we want. WE. CAN'T. STOP. TALKING. ABOUT. JESUS. Jesus comes up in all we talk about and all we do.

If we are watching something on a streaming platform that is questionable, then we will look at each other and decide to turn it off. Besides, I can think of something else we can do other than watching shows. Wait! Sorry! That is for a later chapter. When Tonya texts me an article about what is going on in the world, we will talk about what that means from a biblical perspective. Sometimes we agree. Sometimes we disagree. But we ALWAYS agree in the LORD. Our book is always God's Book, the Bible. Whatever we are discussing or going through, we both love the same Lord, we serve the same King, we surrender to the same Holy Spirit, we arrive at the same book, and we rejoice with the same joy. Marriage is God's idea, and we are all in with Jesus. We walk together as we follow King Jesus, and we love it! You should give it a try!

CONVERSATION STARTERS

1. In what ways can you make known through your marriage that marriage is God's idea? Discuss with one another.

2. What does it mean that you and your spouse are to walk side-by-side in your marriage? What does it not mean?

3. Read Hebrews 13:4. How should marriage be held in honor among all? Discuss with one another.

4. Make a list of ways that you are spiritually unified in marriage. Compare with one another.

Conversation 3

Marriage By the Book

However, let each one of you love his wife as himself, and let the wife see that she respects her husband.
Ephesians 5:33

What role do I play in marriage? What role does my spouse play in marriage? What about my rights in marriage? What about my spouse's responsibilities in marriage? God wants me to be happy in marriage, right?

Marriage is Not a Mirage

There it goes, again! As I write this chapter, while sitting on the balcony of room 1406 in building 2 at the Calypso Resort in Panama City Beach, the mind-numbing noise of a small helicopter circles around me every six minutes and twenty-three seconds. That's right, I clocked it on my phone's stopwatch. Make. It. Stop. O' Lord, deliver me from the Red Helicopter Tours chopper that continues to give folks a ride. Upon arriving at the beach, Tonya and I made a trip to the grocery, and on the way back to the condo, I heard a noise that sounded like a tire had blown out. What was that noise? Of course, it was the same small, red chopper flying overhead. All week I have been hoping that this chattering chopper was a mirage that would disappear as quickly as it appeared. Every minute in America four people walk down the aisle. At first glance, marriage may NOT seem like a mirage, as people are taking a ride to the chapel to get married every minute in America. But, much like that chopper, the ride of marriage for many is over before it begins.

Have you ever read something in the morning that made you spit out your freshly brewed, piping hot sip of coffee or your ice-cold A&W root beer zero with vanilla? What? You have never had an A&W root beer zero with vanilla? I am praying for you. Let's rewind back to the question. Have you ever read a headline that made your heart hurt? The article is heart-breaking and the headline is stunning: "If Bill and Melinda Gates can't make a marriage work, what hope is there for the rest of us?"[x]

The billionaire power couple decided to end their marriage after twenty-seven years. The article stopped short of saying that the Gates divorce is proof that marriage is a mirage; but just barely. Building a case that marriage doesn't work seemed to be the ulterior motive of this article. The article argued that the Gates can afford all the couple counseling in the world, they have more homes than most of us have shoes, they have impacted the world of technology, and their shared passion for philanthropy should have been more than enough to keep them together. From the world's perspective one could easily glean from the Gates divorce: *If a couple with all that going for them can't make marriage work, then we are all doomed before death do us part.*

Is that true? Is marriage some unreliable magic, unbelievable make-believe, uncontrollable mayhem, unattainable mirage, unavoidable mistake, unexplainable myth, or unsolvable mystery? Is there an answer to the mystery of man, woman, and marriage?

One of the most asked questions, not *of* Jesus but *by* Jesus, in Scripture is this: "Have you not read?" Even when Jesus was asked about marriage in Matthew 19, He responded with the question: "Have you not read?" Do you know what that means? Yes! You got it! There *is* a handbook on marriage. No, this handbook on marriage was *not* written by the hand of man, but the hand of God. No, this handbook is *not* merely a good book on marriage, it's God's Book which includes marriage. No, this book is *not* merely a good read by those who read it, it is God reading those who read it. No, this handbook is *not* idle babble, it is the Bible. To misunderstand biblical marriage is to miss the message of the Bible. So, let's take a look at marriage by the book!

Her Role to Submit

He ruled the family with an iron fist. He only did what was pleasing to him and whatever he pleased all the time. She prepared food. She bore children. She had no rights. She had no say. She dared not share her opinion. She was lower than the slaves. Welcome to the married bliss of a home in Rome during the Roman Empire of the first century. He was the ruler, and she was the ruled. Hey ladies, doesn't that give you an overwhelming feeling of being loved? No wonder marriage was on the precipice of disaster. It was in this miserable state of marriage that Jesus the Christ and His church elevated women to a new stature of respect, love, and honor. Let's see God's design for both the roles of husband and wife.

Ladies first. The apostle Paul must have been a gentleman as he addressed the role of the wives first. In Ephesians 5:22-24, Paul wrote:

Wives, submit to your own husbands as to the Lord. For the husband is the head of the wife even as Christ is the head of the church, his body, and is himself its Savior. Now as the church submits to Christ, so also wives should submit in everything to their husbands.

All the ladies be thinking, "What a dirty word! Submit? Me? Never! He doesn't deserve me to submit to him! I know better than him anyway!" You are right in that your husband will never deserve your submission. You are also most likely right that you know better than him. Though, you are wrong in refusing to submit. Yep, it is a sin not to submit. The principle of submission is not punishment for sin. Wives, your role to submit to your husband is not punishment for Eve's sin in the Garden of Eden. Submission was established before the Fall.

Submission was Demonstrated at Creation. Eve was designed to be Adam's partner in every way. Eve was fashioned to be a helper fit for Adam. Eve was not designed to be the head over Adam but to be his helper. From the very beginning, God established authority and submission in the marriage relationship. John Piper said:

> When sin entered the world it ruined the harmony of marriage NOT because it brought headship and submission into existence, but because it twisted man's humble, loving headship into hostile domination in some men and lazy indifference in others. And it twisted woman's intelligent, willing submission into manipulative submission in some women and brazen insubordination in others. Sin didn't create headship and submission; it ruined them and distorted them and made them ugly and destructive.[xi]

After the Fall, there were consequences suffered by both Adam and Eve. Eve would have pain in childbirth. I hear that is still a thing. Ouch. Also, Eve would long to usurp Adam's authority and he would resist by throwing his weight around and demanding her submission. Man, this is happening all the time today. If I had a roll of toilet paper for every time a husband has said to me about his wife, "Pastor, she is not obeying me!" then we would have never experienced a toilet paper shortage. Husbands, she is not called to obey your every command. Wives, you are called to submit to his headship. To conclude that submission to one's husband is punishment for Eve's sin is to also conclude that loving one's wife is punishment for Adam's sin. Both are ludicrous.

Submission Was Articulated by Christ. It is not in there. You will not find it in the New Testament. No, not once. Jesus never stepped outside of God the Father's will. Jesus always submitted to the Father's will. As a result, He who committed no sin was crucified for all sin. In Philippians 2:5-8, we read:

Have this mind among yourselves, which is yours in Christ Jesus, who, though he was in the form of God, did not count equality with God a thing to be grasped, but emptied himself, by taking the form of a servant, being born in the likeness of men. And being found in human form, he humbled himself by becoming obedient to the point of death, even death on a cross.

The principle of submitting to authority defines the kingdom of God.

Submission Is Stipulated for Christians. Paul is not writing to the unchurched but the churched. Paul is not writing to the unsaved but the saved. Paul is not writing to unbelievers but believers. Paul is not writing to non-Christians but Christians. The only way this type of living is possible is through the Holy-Spirit-filled life. Wives who have been saved by Jesus and surrendered to His Lordship are both willing and able to submit to the headship of their husbands.

What Submission Means. Submission is a voluntary attitude of giving in, cooperating, assuming responsibility, and carrying a burden. Wives are to recognize that God has given the husband responsibility for leading the family. Two bosses never work; neither at work nor at home. Submission is a decision. It's a decision on the part of the wife to accept the role in the family that God has given her. By the way, wives, you are not to submit to every man, but only to your husband.

What Submission Doesn't Mean. Listen up husbands! Submission doesn't mean that your wife is your slave. Submission doesn't mean that a wife is inferior to her husband. Submission doesn't mean that a wife should follow her husband's lead if it is sinful. Submission doesn't mean that the wife has no value or opinion.

Remember, God's answer to the anti-authority age in which we live is submission. Our submission is not about our rights. Our submission is not about their (the people to whom we are to submit) responsibilities. Let's not be like Peter who asked the Lord, after he received his marching orders, "What about this man?" Peter was referring to John. Don't let *whataboutism* rule the day, but follow the One who is risen. Jesus' paraphrased response to Peter went like this: *What is that to you? You, Peter, follow me.* Submission is not about the character of the one to whom we submit. Submission is about the command of God. Submission is all about God. In 1 Peter 3:1, the Holy Spirit reminds us:

> *Likewise, wives, be subject to your own husbands, so that even if some do not obey the word, they may be won...*

Steve and Kathy Lee

He couldn't wait to tell me his story. When I heard his testimony, I was shook! As I listened, I was mentally inserting at different times during his story, "No he didn't! No she didn't!" He was sitting on the couch in my office when all of a sudden he sprung to his feet and shouted, "Pastor, I got born-again at fifty-two years old!" His wife was sitting next to him wearing a HUGE smile.

Steve and Kathy had been married twenty years when Steve got saved. Kathy prayed for Steve constantly for twenty years. Twenty years! Not only did she pray for him, she also submitted to him. I could never tell it like Steve, but here is a paraphrase of his testimony:

> Like every other Sunday morning, I woke up that Sunday morning with no plans to go to church. Kathy had been going to church without me for twenty years. Why should this Sunday be any different? I was sitting and drinking a cup of coffee when I saw Kathy, or so I thought, walk by already dressed to go to

church. I thought, "She is beautiful." Later I realized that this was most likely an angel.

I walked around the house looking for Kathy. She wasn't in the living room, bathroom, kitchen, or the bedroom. As I walked in the bedroom, I walked over to the closet and started putting on clothes. Before I knew what was happening, I was dressed for church. I walked into the kitchen, and there Kathy sat. She wasn't dressed for church and her hair was still in rollers. She looked at me and said, "Why are you dressed like that?" I replied, "I guess I am going to church with you today." She jumped from the table and readied herself for church. Kathy could hardly believe her ears.

When we arrived at the church, we walked in and found our seat. At some point that morning, I ended up at the church altar feeling like I was in a whirlwind. I said, "God I think I know why I'm here. You brought me in." My next thought was to tell him I'm sorry for all the rotten things I've done and then I said, "I think I need your help." BOOM! God gave me His Holy Spirit and changed me forever. It was April 18, 2010, and I have been on fire for Jesus ever since that day.

Because Kathy submitted to her husband as unto the Lord and for twenty years prayed without ceasing for him to be saved, Steve got saved! Wives, let this be an encouragement for you that even your lost husband can be saved. Yes. He. Can. Wives, be subject to your husband and if he is not saved, he may be won.

Her Role to Help

Tonya loves to clean and keep the house. When she thinks of what I love to do, study and write sermons, she says, "I can't even!"

SAM & TONYA GREER

When I think of what she loves to do, clean and keep the house up, I say, "I can't even!" Of all the chores, the one chore Tonya loathes is laundry. I agree with her. Laundry is loathsome. Raise your hand if you like doing laundry. Laundry was not in God's perfect creation. I can prove it. Adam and Eve got clothes after they sinned which means laundry is a result of the Fall. Before the Fall, Adam and Eve were both naked and felt no shame. Can you imagine a world with no laundry and husband and wife both naked all the time? I'll take that all day every day and twice on Sunday!

A wife's role as helper means "to complete" her husband, not "to compete" with her husband. At the same time, the role of helper doesn't mean a wife must do everything in the house while the husband does what he likes outside the house. A husband and wife are a team. A married couple are in a partnership together. Take a team approach to marriage. Make a plan. Talk through what you are passionate about and decide together who will be responsible for what. Let your giftedness from the Holy Spirit be your guide. Just keep it in the boundary of husband as the head and wife as the helper.

Tonya is gifted in keeping up with our finances down to the penny. I am not. So, Tonya is the one who keeps track of our finances and balances our account. Yes, you heard right! I did say *our* finances and *our* account. If you are married, it is appropriate to have his and hers this and that, but it is *not* appropriate to have his and her accounts. You need to understand that "my" money becomes "our" money once you say "I do." More on that in a later conversation.

On a monthly basis, Tonya and I discuss how much we will pay toward this or that how much we will save, how much we will give, how much is left over to buy shoes, and together we make those decisions. When there is a call to make one way or the other, as the husband, I make that call; however, I always hear Tonya's opinion—always. A husband is the head and the wife is to help her husband, not harm him, not humiliate him, and not hurt him.

His Role to Love

I'll never forget that day. I'll never forget that conversation. I'll never forget that moment. The Holy Spirit made it clear that Tonya was the one He had chosen for me. God spoke to me louder than audibly and in the most unusual of ways. One of my friends, Robert Knight, got in my face and said:

> What are you thinking? You better not let Tonya get away. None of us deserve a girl like that. You better get your act together and ask her to marry you.

I was speechless. I was shocked. I didn't expect that coming from Robert. If you knew Robert, then you wouldn't have expected that either. What a timely word from a timeless God through a "for such a time as this" friend! I quickly proposed. Tonya was shocked. I am thankful that she said, Yes!

Who said "I love you" first? You or your spouse? I was the first to say, "I think I love you." What is that? What was I thinking when I said, *I think*? Obviously, I wasn't. Tonya was the first to say, "I love you." Husbands, God isn't concerned with who says it first; rather, He is concerned with who does it first. Don't just be sayers of the word *love* but be doers of the word *love*. In fact, God commands husbands to first and foremost love their wives. In Ephesians 5:25-28, and 33 Paul penned:

> *Husbands,* **love** *your wives as Christ* **loved** *the church and gave himself up for her, that he might sanctify her, having cleansed her by the washing of water with the word, so that he might present the church to himself in splendor, without spot or wrinkle or any such thing, that she might be holy and without blemish. In the same way husbands should* **love** *their wives as their own bodies. He who* **loves** *his wife* **loves** *himself...let each of you* **love** *his wife as himself...*

The word "love" is mentioned six times in these five verses. "Love" here refers to an unconditional, no strings attached, expecting nothing-in-return, unrelenting kind of love that is driven by our will and actions, not our feelings. The world says that love is about feeling. The Word says that love is about committing. Feelings will fail you, but committing will free you. Jesus didn't *feel like* dying on the cross for your sins and mine, but love compelled Him to take up His cross. Now, husbands, it is time for us to take up our cross, not our crown, and love our wives as Christ loved the church!

Husbands, we were designed by our Creator to love our wives. Tim Keller said:

> The fish must honor its design. It is designed for water, not for land. Real freedom is not living without restrictions. It's about finding the right ones.[xii]

The primary role of a husband in the marriage relationship is to love his wife. God's design says so. How are husbands to love their wives?

Love Your Wife Continuously. God is not passing out a license for husbands to stop loving their wives. If you are a follower of Jesus, the Holy Spirit will empower you to love your wife non-stop even when it is hard. I have heard more than one husband say:

> I don't love my wife anymore. I deserve to be happy. I have found my soul mate elsewhere. My wife has let herself go. She doesn't meet my needs.

Don't love your wife because of who she is, love her because of who the Trinity is. Husbands, we are to love our wives as God's daughter, Jesus' co-heir, and the Holy Spirit's temple, not just as our wives while we are on earth.

Love Your Wife Sacrificially. Me, myself and I destroy more marriages than anything else. Loving your wife selfishly is a ton easier than loving her sacrificially. Men, when was the last time you gave up something that meant a lot to you in order to bless your wife? How can we "give ourselves up for her" if we are not willing to give up something to bless her? Marriage is a never-ending, life-long lesson in saying no to me, myself, and I. Men, Jesus gave himself up sacrificially for you. Jesus bought you at the ultimate price by shedding His blood on the cross and breathing His last so you could breathe at last. Is He getting what He paid for? Husbands, when was the last time you said no to yourself? When was the last time you should have said no to self for the sake of saying yes to your wife? Husbands, loving your wife sacrificially should cost you something, but it will pay off. Love your wife sacrificially!

Love Your Wife Strategically. Jesus' focus is on His church, not Himself. Jesus focuses on the church in order to present the church to Himself as His perfect Bride! Husbands, where is your focus? Do you love your wife enough to focus on her more than yourself? Do you love your wife enough to focus on her needs more than your own needs? Husbands, do for your wife what God did for you in Jesus. Focus on her. God never takes His eyes off of us. We may lose sight of Him, but He never loses sight of us. At some point in your relationship, you couldn't take your eyes off of your wife. Make the commitment now to not take your heart off of her.

Love Your Wife Tenderly. Nourish her. Pay attention to your wife. Cherish her. Paul is not thinking only of supplying your wife with barely enough to survive but lavishing on her the care and attention we give to our own bodies. Do you understand that there is never one moment that Christ does not tenderly watch over His Body, the church? We are under His constant surveillance because He cares for us. In that way, love your wives! Husbands, you shouldn't have to worry about another man giving your wife the attention that you should be giving her. Pay attention to her! I never have to worry about another man giving Tonya the attention that she is not getting from me.

I Never Have to Worry About Another Man Giving Tonya the Attention That She is Not Getting From Me

His Role to Lead

Styles come and go. Parachute pants parachuted out of style as quickly as they parachuted in style. Thank you, Aunt Trudy, for convincing mom that a ten-year old fifth grader needed a pair of parachute pants for the first day of school in 1984. I am not bitter about my buddy Rick Deaton being the only kid in fifth grade with a Michael Jackson Thriller jacket. No, I harbor no bitterness at all. I told bitterness to "Just beat it, beat it, no one wants to be defeated."[xiii]

Yes, styles come and go, but being a gentleman never goes out of style. Husbands, we should open doors, pull out chairs, offer to carry things, and insist on paying. We fulfill our role as the leader of the family when we lead by example. That's right, God expects you to lead your wife and your family. Men, we have the primary role of leadership in the family. We must not abuse this role, be absent from this role, or be passive in this role. Husbands are responsible and accountable for the spiritual, physical and emotional welfare of his family. He is to put his family before himself. Lead like the Lord Jesus. Servant leadership is the way of the Savior.

Ladies, Marry a Man Who Wants to Be a Husband, Not Just a Man Who Wants a Wife. Men, Marry a Woman Who Wants to Be in a Marriage, Not Just One Who wants a Wedding.

Men, marriage is more than wanting a wife. Ladies, marriage is more than wanting a wedding. So, ladies, marry a man who wants to be a husband, not just a man who wants a wife. Men, marry a woman who wants to be in a marriage, not just one who wants a wedding.

She Says

Wow. Wouldn't you love to be married to a man who lived up to all of those rolls! Me too! Oh wait, I am! I don't like to brag or anything, but I hit the jackpot with my hubs. I've made lots of mistakes in marriage, but there's one thing I can say I've done right. I pray for my man. Prayer is the most under used power there is. We often wear ourselves out thinking of ways we can handle or fix a certain situation. What we can say to our kids to make them stop being a certain way? Who we can confide in to get the perfect remedy or vent to? But what we really need to be doing is going to our knees and letting God fight for us.

I remember as a teen, constantly hearing stories of affairs and cheating. Maybe because my favorite TV show was Beverly Hills 90210. Yikes. But I knew as a young girl that would not be my story. I do remember praying for my man even then. I told God everything I wanted. And I had some really high standards. When I met Sam, the only demand he met was that he was really good looking. It made me weak at the knees. He was not marriage material. Even though I knew from the moment I laid eyes on him that he was THE ONE. (Unfortunately, he didn't realize that for months.)

I am no expert by any means, but Sam and I do have a great marriage. I want to pass on some tips for wives to give you some insight into how you can also have a fun and fulfilling marriage.

Top on my list, PRAY FOR YOUR MAN. As I said, I started praying as a teenager, before meeting THE ONE was even on my radar. In fact, at one point I was having so much fun casually dating that I asked God to hold off on sending THE ONE. But when I finally did meet him, he didn't meet all the criteria. Yes, he was (and still is) very good looking, drove a big, cool truck and could tear up a dance floor, but he also had A LOT of girls that liked him, stood me up numerous times, and didn't manage what little money he had very well. Oh, and he had been working on a bachelor's degree for way more than four years. I had also gotten radically saved a few months after meeting Sam, and he wasn't even remotely following God.

    I don't tell you all this to bash my man. I certainly wasn't perfect (still not). I was terribly insecure, and I loved to spend my weekends on the dance floor at whatever night club was open the latest and had a bouncer that would let in underaged girls. We were both finding our way. But I did know what I wanted, and I wanted Sam. So, I started praying, "God take this from my heart." I didn't want to feel this way about someone who didn't reciprocate. Y'all, that was just torture. But God didn't take it away. I went off to college pining away for this guy who couldn't even remember when we had plans to go to the mall while I was home visiting.

    God didn't answer my prayers immediately like I wanted, but He did eventually answer them. And y'all, I got it all. God changed his heart. I did not. We can't change anyone. Only God can. You can argue all you want about all of your husband's faults. I'm sure your husband can do the same about you. But what's undeniable is the power of prayer. Commit to praying *until*. Until you have everything you want. Or until God changes your heart. And then pray some more—there is always something to pray about. Because the whole point of prayer is not to get what you want. It's for God to change YOU. He doesn't always answer the way we like. He isn't our genie in a bottle. But we have to trust that His ways are better than ours. Sure, I got the man of my dreams, but I didn't know that would land me the role of preacher's wife in the first few years of marriage. See, that's how God changed me. We've got to trust Him. He gave me a desire I never knew I had. Being a pastor's wife has been the greatest blessing of my life. I love it and can't imagine any other life. So, get on your knees for your family. There are powerful forces out there ready to tear down our families, but we have the greatest weapon. You are not on your own.

Next, know your role in your family. I know. You don't like that submit word. I don't always either. Sometimes I pout for a minute when I don't get my way. Which is a very bad example, so don't do it. It's very manipulative and let me tell you, if you want the most dreadful, toxic marriage (or relationship), go ahead and get what you want by manipulating your way there. We all do it, so don't say you would never. Manipulation can be very effective, but it will destroy all good things. Your spouse will grow to resent and even hate you after enough of it. I've had to catch myself more times than I want to admit. But we have to own it. Go apologize. Do it now. And cut it out.

God gave us roles. They are clearly listed in the Bible. He calls men to lead, and we have to let them. I hate TV shows where they make fun of parents. I will make my girls turn it off, and they know it. I'm thankful they can now recognize when the world is teaching them to make fun of the family unit. To me, it's absolutely demonic. Sam has often said the break-down of the family unit is the reason for so much destruction in our world today. Satan is after our families. The world teaches our men to stand down and let women do everything. They praise men for watching porn and playing video games while the wives run the house and manage the kids. If you are married to a man who does that, go back to my first tip on having a successful marriage. Start praying for your man.

Respect your husband. Does that mean you love and agree with everything he does and says? No. But you have to respect him and teach your children to as well. If you really want a toxic family, bad mouth your husband, and do it in front of your children. Again, Scripture tells us that He chose the man as the head of the house. If you don't like the way he does it, then get on your knees. You can't change him, but God can. He needs a woman behind him praying. Every great man has a powerful prayer warrior behind him. He can't do it alone. He needs YOU! That's why Adam got Eve. God chose you for your man!

Ladies, take care of yourself. If you are exhausted, sleep deprived, overwhelmed and empty, you have nothing to give everyone else. Does that mean you have to go into debt on surgery, hair, and clothes? No. Make the best of what you have. Say *no* to things so you have time and money for yourself. Your man wants to see you looking good. There's no shame in fixing your hair and makeup and showing your man a little skin. Flirt with your man! They love it! They eat it up! Especially in front of other people. Praise him when he isn't even listening. Yes, there is something about him to praise! Focus on that!

And this is where Sam wants me to encourage you to do it. You know, the thing us women like to put off. I'm rolling my eyes as I type this (*not AT you but WITH you*) because I totally get what you are thinking. Guys just need it so try to make some effort. I'm not getting into gory details because they aren't necessary and my parents will read this, so just go with me here.

And date your man. I know it's hard to do when money is tight and/or you have kids at home. Those kids do get older and one day will be gone. You need to enjoy your marriage because it will last way beyond having kids in the house. He is your forever companion, so spend time nourishing that relationship. Sam and I go to the movies every Friday night. We love to just sit there. I get all dressed up. In my ripped jeans. Jeans are my dress up clothes these days. And flip flops. I've had the same pair for four years, but I take a minute to paint my toes so they are still cute.

As Sam said earlier, I love to keep house. When I was a teenager, my mom cleaned houses as a living, and I'd go with her. I loved it. Not just because I like to clean but because I also love being with my momma. So maybe that's why I associate cleaning with fun. Who knows? But I can spend hours tinkering around the house picking up and cleaning. And yes, much to Sam's dismay, we do wear clothes at our house despite my aversion to laundry.

I know not everyone loves to clean the way I do, and that's ok. I'm home more and have the time, but not everyone has that. But I do encourage you to make a little effort to make things nice for him when he comes home. I hate to cook! I mean HATE it. Everyone in our house wants something different. I end up making four meals and all the dishes take nearly an hour to clean up. Arg. But I do try. A little. At least a few nights a week. Again, these are things that you can negotiate in your marriage but they are necessary things. So, take some time to divvy out chores so everyone's needs are being met. You'd be surprised how negotiations can work for you. No one person needs to carry the whole load.

We all have a role to play in our own family unit. The question you need to ask yourself is: are you contributing to a healthy family unit or are you contaminating it? Just know your kids are watching. You are shaping their lives. Do you want them to have healthy, biblical marriages? The best thing you can do is let them live inside a healthy one, and pray for their spouses.

I've always had A TON of hair. My mom told me when I was very young that she didn't have a lot of hair, so while she was pregnant with me, she prayed that I would have a lot of hair. I thought that was pretty cool, so while pregnant, I did the same for my girls. And here we are. Three heads FULL of hair. Yes, our drains are ALWAYS clogged.

After our girls were born (with a head full of hair), I loved to sit and rock them. God clearly gave them the hair I asked for, so why not ask for more? I started praying for their spouses while I rocked them. I STILL pray for their spouses. I pray for the parents raising my girls' husbands because they are raising my future sons-in-law. I was never able to give my man a son, and it haunts me sometimes. He loves to throw a ball, and anytime we are going to be around a group of men or teenage boys, he brings a ball they can throw. It's so cute. So, I've told God He needs to send us the most magnificent sons-in-laws ever. I can't wait, I'm already excited! It's gonna be fantastic! So be praying for those spouses. God just might give you your heart's desire! Bless your kids with praying parents. I truly believe God will honor it!

I'm a never-ending optimist. God can fix anything! There's no end He won't go to for you! You can have a happy marriage! It will never be perfect. But the grass is greener where you water it. So, stay in your own yard, and water your own grass.

xoxo

Marriage Is a Mirror

What. A. Word. Boo Boo. So good! Husbands and wives, we don't deserve to be happy, but we must desire to be holy. You see, marriage is a mirror that reflects the Holy Trinity. God the Father, God the Son and God the Holy Spirit give us a picture of how the marriage relationship must be equal and ordered. God created marriage as a permanent relationship to last till death. God created marriage whereby husband and wife are equal, just as the three Persons of the One God are equal. Jesus, God the Son, rules over the church while also submitting to the Father's will. Likewise, God created marriage with authority to be exercised with love by the husband and submission to be given willingly by the wife.

Marriage is a mirror that reflects the gospel of the Lord Jesus Christ. Every Christian marriage is proclaiming the gospel every day. Paul wrote, in Ephesians 5:32:

This mystery is profound, and I am saying that it refers to Christ and the church.

Goodness! Your marriage and mine exists to proclaim the message of the good news! How awesome is that! Is your marriage mirroring the gospel? When others look in on your marriage, do they see grace? Is your marriage making the invisible grace of God visible? Is your marriage grace-based? Husbands and wives, if you will love and submit respectfully, then your marriage will mirror the gospel of our Maker. So, never base your obedience on your spouse's performance.

Marriage is a Mission Field

Church, don't allow your ministry to replace your marriage. Your marriage is your ministry. Understand that God expects you to stand under the whole armor of God as you fight for marriage, including your own marriage. Don't think for one minute that Paul unintentionally inserted the armor of God text after the text on marriage and family. He put it there for a reason. Why? We are at war and it is not *The War of the Roses*! It's not a war against man and woman. Oh no, this is a far more sinister enemy. Paul wrote in Ephesians 6:10-13:

Finally, be strong in the Lord and in the strength of his might. Put on the whole armor of God, that you may be able to stand against the schemes of the devil. For we do not wrestle against flesh and blood, but against the rulers, against the authorities, against the cosmic powers over this present darkness, against the spiritual forces of evil in the heavenly places. Therefore take up the whole armor of God, that you may be able to withstand in the evil day, and having done all, to stand firm.

Is Paul chasing spiritual rabbits here? What is going on? Why is Paul writing about the armor of God? Do husbands and wives need to protect themselves from each other like the married assassins working for adversarial agencies in the movie *Mr. and Mrs. Smith*?

We have a real enemy. A real evil enemy. An enemy who desires to kill, steal and destroy marriage. Satan is relentless in his efforts to destroy marriage. He will not stop. He will continue to prowl around like a roaring lion until Jesus comes again. But, we have armor that will enable us to stand and stand firm.

How does this armor protect us? Is it magic? Is it state-of-the-art? You might be thinking, "I certainly hope this armor is stronger than the Empire's stormtrooper armor." What is up with the stormtrooper's armor? Can the Empire not afford to give them armor other than plastic? No, this armor is not like the stormtrooper's armor. Each and every piece of the armor is the Lord Jesus Christ Himself.

Think about each piece of the armor of God. The belt of truth represents Jesus being the Truth. The breastplate of righteousness represents Jesus as our righteousness. The gospel shoes of peace represent Jesus as the Prince of Peace. The shield of faith represents Jesus as the Faithful and True witness. The helmet of salvation represents Jesus as the Savior. The sword of the Spirit represents Jesus as the Word of God. Each and every piece of the armor is the Lord Jesus. Jesus alone defeated Satan. Jesus alone fights our battles. Jesus alone saves. Jesus alone. Jesus alone. Jesus alone.

Marrieds Discipling Marrieds. I challenge you to look for a younger married couple that you and your spouse can pour into. Check in on them once per week. Take them out to eat or have them in your home for a meal once a month. Get to know them. Listen to them. Share struggles with them. Let them know that a good marriage is when each person says "no" to self. Marriage is not only to be transformational, but incarnational. Investing in a younger married couple is what incarnational marriage is all about. Pray about which younger married couple God would have you and your spouse invest. Talk about a plan to encourage them weekly and monthly.

Also, I challenge you to ask an older married couple to mentor you as a married couple. A strong biblical principle is for every believer to have a Barnabas (an encourager), a Paul (a mentor), and a Timothy to disciple. Why not apply this to marriage? Satan's target is your marriage and your family. Married couples, arm yourself with a Barnabas, Paul and Timothy. At the same time, be a Barnabas, Paul and Timothy to other marrieds.

CONVERSATION STARTERS

1. What are the roles of a husband and wife in marriage? In what ways are you fulfilling your role in your marriage? In what ways are you not?

2. Wives, ask your husband to tell you the times when he feels respected and honored by you the most. Ask him about the times when he doesn't.

3. Husbands, ask your wife to tell you the times when she feels loved by you the most. Ask her about the times when she doesn't.

4. Pray about a younger married couple in whom you can invest and an older couple who can invest in you.

Conversation 4

Making Marriage Matter, Matters

Let marriage be held in honor among all... **Hebrews 13:4**

Does marriage really matter? What value does marriage hold in America? What impact does marriage have on American culture? What does it look like when marriage is held in honor? Can a case be made for marriage being held in honor among all?

Marriage Is a Marathon

I gave the late Dr. Jerry Barlow ample opportunity to refuse my entrance into the doctoral program. I did. I told him that I was not smart enough to earn a PhD. No way. He said to me, "You don't have to be smart enough. You just need to be stubborn enough." Perseverance and stick-to-itiveness are the keys to finishing any PhD. Upon completing the grueling and tedious six plus year doctoral program, I decided to start another arduous one-year program; training for a marathon.

SAM & TONYA GREER

It was December 2014. I graduated with a PhD and determined that I would celebrate by training for a December 2015 marathon. Why? I don't know. There was just one problem. I was not running at all. Zero. Zilch. Nada. Not even from the couch to the fridge. So, I did what any person who is a glutton for punishment would do. I trained for and ran a 5k in January 2015. Then, I trained for and ran a half marathon in April of 2015. Finally, I trained for and ran a marathon in December of 2015. All in one year. No, I don't recommend that plan. My Yelp review of that plan would be about half a star. Yep, that's right half a star at best on Yelp.

On December 12, 2015, I finished the Rocket City Marathon in Huntsville, Alabama, at the age of forty-one. I ran two marathons in one: (1) my first marathon and (2) my last marathon. No more marathons for me. Please. One is plenty. Oh, that twenty-six plus mile run was really not all that fun. No, it really wasn't. It was painful and drainful all at the same time. No more marriages for me, BUT for a very different reason. I am having way too much fun being married to Tonya!

Long marathons are made up of small moments. In any given marathon, there are at least twenty-six small moments realized by runners as they cross each mile marker. But there are also countless other moments had along the way. Some moments are not so good. Like the moment both of my calf muscles cramped up at mile eighteen during the Rocket City marathon. And some moments are good. Like when I crossed the thirteen-mile marker where Braydee, Belle, and Tonya were standing and cheering. What about the whole year of training moments in preparation for the marathon? Sure, we have time for me to tell you about one such moment.

Training for a marathon consists of bitterly cold runs, humid and hot runs, early morning runs, mid-afternoon runs, evening runs, late-night runs, short runs, and long runs. Remembering all the training runs is next to impossible; however, there is one training run I will never forget.

GOSPEL CONVERSATIONAL MARRIAGE

We visit my mother-in-law in Mississippi several times each year. The neighborhood where she resides offers a respectable two-mile run out to the main road. One hot, humid, summer morning, I took off on a four-mile run.

Running in the summer humidity of south-central Mississippi is like running in a sauna. As I was running—well, *running* may be a stretch. As I was jogging—well, *jogging* may be a leap. As I was rogging (a combination of running and jogging)—well, *rogging* may be an exaggeration. As I was walking—again, *walking* may even be up for debate. As I was moving, pouring sweat, panting for oxygen, and thirsting for something, anything, in liquid form, it happened.

Although I was moving slowly uphill for the final quarter-mile of a four-mile run, anyone could tell that I was intentionally trying to exercise. Wearing earbuds was clear evidence that I was listening to jogging tunes. Wearing running shorts, a half-marathon t-shirt, and running shoes was clearer evidence that I was attempting to run. Wearing the painful expression on my face was the clearest evidence that I was trying to jog. Being outside in the middle of a hot, humid day, it was painfully obvious that I was exercising.

Blanketed by the blazing sun and looking up from the bottom of the hill, I noticed an SUV coming over the crest. Immediately, the lady driving began to slow down. The next couple of minutes seemed to be right out of a movie as if everything was moving in slow motion. You know, like a Guy Ritchie directed film when the action slows down. Look, there is no debate. Ritchie's directed version of the Sherlock Holmes franchise are some of the best movies in cinema history. You don't agree? Come at me!

As everything seemed like it was in slow motion, the SUV pulled further over to my side of the road. It was so close I could feel the cool conditioned air sweep over my face as the driver's side backseat window rolled down. As the refreshing, crisp, cool air enveloped my blistering, red-hot face, an outstretched arm extended from the deep freezer-like coolness of the vehicle.

SAM & TONYA GREER

In the hand of the outstretched arm was a mouth-watering 20-ounce soft drink. The thirst-quenching drink was covered with small drops of ice cascading down the sides and off the bottom of the bottle. The melting drops of ice almost sizzled as it touched down onto the scorching hot Mississippi pavement.

The sweet, middle-aged lady holding the soft drink, as if practiced a thousand times on a track relay team, handed me that cold, enticing, bottle in stride. I looked at her eyeball-to-eyeball and said,

"Thank you."

Being undeniably thirsty, I truly meant it. As the grateful words left my lips, I heard the two ladies in the front seat say,

"Wait, stop!"

I stopped. The SUV stopped. The lady who handed me the soft drink asked,

"Could you open this bottle for me?"

What?

Could you open this bottle for me?

The only thing worse than running in the Mississippi humidity was holding that ice-cold soft drink, only to open it and hand it back to its owner. As the SUV pulled away, I heard the ladies in the front seat laughing and saying,

"He thought that drink was for him!"

Marriage is like a long marathon full of small moments. Good moments. Bad moments. Memorable moments. Forgettable moments.

GOSPEL CONVERSATIONAL MARRIAGE

Funny moments. Not so funny moments. Hurtful moments. Helpful moments. Hopeful moments. Graceful moments. Not so graceful moments. Grace-filled moments. Not so grace-filled moments. *Again, who stops a person from exercising and asks him or her to open a drink for them? Who does that? I am not still bitter. Sorry, let's get back to the moments.* Grateful moments. Ungrateful moments. Planned moments. Unplanned moments. Sad moments. Glad moments. Teachable moments. Seen moments. Unseen moments. Big moments. Small moments. The marathon of marriage is made up of many moments.

Don't underestimate moments. We are so busy trying to get to whatever is "next" we miss the moment. Moments are momentous. In the summertime, one of my favorite moments is when I get to take Tonya a frozen Outshine Raspberry Fruit Bar while she is laying out at our pool. *Y'all, I was today years old (the day I wrote this paragraph) when I learned that "raspberry" is spelled with a "p." Who knew? I didn't.* Back to another moment.

Another favorite moment is when I see Tonya for the first time on Sunday mornings. I rise early on Sundays and get to the church to pray and read over sermon notes. I don't see Tonya until around 10:55 a.m. when I walk into the worship center for the third worship service of the day. The room is filled with people, but I only have one person in my eyesight—Tonya. I look forward to seeing what Tonya is wearing each Sunday morning. She. Is. Hot. I love taking the seat next to her and giving her a kiss.

The key is to not miss the moments in marriage for the marathon of marriage. Make more, not less, of your marriage moments. Making your marriage matter is all about making the moments in your marriage matter. By the way, making marriage moments matter, matters. You'll start making the most of your marriage when you start making more of your marriage moments. The best way to make *more of* your marriage moments is to make *more* marriage moments.

STOP reading NOW, and GO make a marriage moment with your spouse. Wives, go compliment your husband. Husbands, go out of your way to serve your wife. Yes, now! I'll be here when you get back.

Welcome back! You might be thinking, why is it important to make much of marriage moments? Husbands and wives, if we are not making marriage matter in our homes, then we can't expect marriage to matter outside the home. God's Word is clear in Hebrews 13:4:

Let marriage be held in honor among all.

Marriage is to be valued. The Greek word used for "honor" is *timios* which can be transliterated as *"precious, valued, of great worth, held in honor, highly respected, prized, pertaining to being of exceptional value."*[xiv] Marriage is not to be redefined, but respected. Marriage is not to be re-evaluated, but valued.

Marathons are not run by all, but marathons are, more likely than not, respected by all. Marriage is not required of all, but it must be respected by all. God holds marriage in high regard as He refers to His church as the Bride of Christ. God describes the gathering of believers in heaven as the Marriage Supper of the Lamb. God calls us to "put on our wedding clothes" and ready ourselves for Christ's coming as a bride readies herself for her wedding. Paul the Apostle writes of marriage in the context of Christ and His church. If God and His Word have such a high view of marriage, then shouldn't we and our words? Shouldn't all and their words?

Making Marriage Matter, Matters

Have you ever wondered why pure religion is described as visiting orphans and widows? In James 1:27, the Bible says:

Religion that is pure and undefiled before God, the Father, is this: to visit orphans and widows in their affliction, and to keep oneself unstained from the world.

The Holy Spirit, through James, in these two statements describes the conduct and character of a follower of Christ. Pertaining to character, believers are to keep themselves *unstained from the world*. What a reminder to stay close to God and remain clean before God. Stay in His Word for as long as you stay in this world. The Bible has no equal. The Bible has no sequel. The Bible has no rival. The Bible has gone viral. Follow that science!

As it relates to conduct, believers are to visit orphans and widows. What does it mean to *visit* them? Hang out with them? Take them some soup? Order them some Grubhub? The word transliterated as "visit" in the Greek is *episkeptomal* which means: *"to look after," "care for," "be concerned about," "take care of," "to make a careful inspection,"* and *"to go and see a person with helpful intent."*[xv]

Why would orphans and widows need such potential help? Both orphans and widows have one thing in common, the marriage in their family is no more. Death separated the orphan from his or her parents and the widow from her husband. Without marriage in place, the orphan and widow had no way to provide for themselves in the culture of James' day. Don't you see? The absence of marriage mattered two thousand years ago and had a huge impact on orphans and widows. In their affliction, they had no foundational structure (marriage) for relief and support. The whole idea here is for believers to sacrificially love and help one another with no strings attached. That is, to help others while expecting NOTHING in return.

Marriage mattered two thousand years ago in a real, tangible way. Just ask the orphans and widows. Well, what about today? We are living in a different day. We have seen more opportunity for the less fortunate than in previous centuries. Can a case *still* be made for marriage to be held in honor among all?

I am convinced that there is a direct correlation between marriage rates and the rates of crime,

physical health, financial stability, abortion, fostering, sex-trafficking, and education.

Marriage matters more today than ever. In research obtained for this book, I am convinced that there is a direct correlation between marriage rates and the rates of crime, physical health, financial stability, abortion, fostering, sex-trafficking, and education. Marriage still matters and the decline of marriage rates affects the whole of any society.

"If we care about kids, we should care about marriage. Let's not pretend that we have abandoned marriage for the benefit of children. We have done it solely for the freedom of adults."

Marriage still matters to children. In an article titled, "Forget Race or Class, Marriage is the Big Social Divide," *The Spectator* reported that underachieving children and child poverty have a common denominator. The common denominator is not race, class, or gender; but rather, the state of marriage and its sinking rates. The article surmised:

> They've (marriage rates) been steadily collapsing since the 1970's. Not just declining but falling off a cliff. Even at the height of the second world war, one of its previous lowest points, the male marriage rate was almost triple what it is today. We claim to value our families but imagine the response if something we truly cared about, like employment rates, were doing the same. People tell me that talk of marriage is moralising and uncomfortable and revert to the importance of 'stability' to children instead. But let's call a spade a spade. There is no other form of relationship that offers anywhere near

the same level of stability in any thriving culture in the whole of human history. If we care about kids, we should care about marriage. Alarmed wedding bells should be ringing and ringing hard...Let's not pretend then that we have abandoned marriage for the benefit of children. We have done it solely for the freedom of adults.[xvi]

Adults, that is in our face! So convicting. So true. We need to stop kidding ourselves. Adults have not forsaken marriage for the *sake* of the kids. We have freed ourselves of the bonds of marriage so that we can be *free*. God have mercy on us! Think about it. Secular media celebrates the fact that celebrities jump on and off the marry-go-round of marriage like they are at an amusement park. Meanwhile, the rest of us on social media are tempted to join the world in making a mockery of marriage. Affirmative, there is an ongoing, world-wide pandemic, and it is not COVID-19. It is an ever-widening and far reaching disregard for MATTHEW 19:

Therefore a man shall leave his father and his mother and hold fast to his wife, and the two shall become one flesh.

Not only does the decline of marriage have a negative impact on the education of children and child poverty, but it also impacts abortion rates. According to the National Abortion Federation:

Most women getting abortions (83%) are unmarried; 67% have never married, and 16% are separated, divorced, or widowed. Married women are significantly less likely than unmarried women to resolve unintended pregnancies through abortion.[xvii]

How many fewer abortions would've happened had more marriages happened?

The decay of marriage and family has also left its mark on the human trafficking of children. According to Thomas Reuters Foundation:

> Without family, U.S. children in foster care are easy prey for human traffickers. Children removed from unfit families and put in foster care are terrifyingly vulnerable to being trafficked. Eighty-eight percent of children who were victims of sex trafficking were in the care of child welfare.[xviii]

Marriage and family are essential, not optional.

Moreover, unhealthy family units play a significant role in the trafficking of children. A study on high-risk groups for trafficking human beings reported:

> Family-related factors emerged as the key group of both risk and resilience factors related to the trafficking of children. Among those, stable structure of the family unit paired with a good, trust-based relationship between parent and child, which includes a healthy level of parental monitoring, were found to be the most powerful resilience factors...As regards risk factors related to the family situation, a situation of family breakdown was considered especially important as it often manifested in neglect, abuse, or abandonment of children.[xix]

How many fewer children would've been sex trafficked had more marriages happened and if more marriages are continued to happen?

Marriage is work, but the way God intended it, it works! Marriage works to procreate children, provide for children, and protect children. Marriage still matters to children. Go ahead and ask them!

"Marriage remains America's strongest anti-poverty, anti-crime, pro-health institution."

Marriage should still matter to everyone. Including children, marriage should still matter to everyone. The breakdown of marriage affects everyone, even the unmarried. The Heritage Foundation explained:

> Decades of statistics have shown that, on average, married couples have better physical health, more financial stability, and greater social mobility than unmarried people. Other studies show that the children of those couples are more likely to experience higher academic performance, emotional maturity, and financial stability than children who don't have both parents in the home. Studies show divorce and unwed childbearing cost taxpayers over $110 billion each year. But the real victims are children. Children raised in single-parent homes are statistically more likely to abuse drugs and alcohol, exhibit poor social behaviors, and commit violent crimes. And when it comes to fighting poverty there is no better weapon than marriage. In fact, marriage reduces the probability of child poverty by 80%. Marriage remains America's strongest anti-poverty, anti-crime, and pro-health institution.[xx]

A strong case can be made for real life practical benefits of biblical marriage. Sadly, marriage is more dismissed than it is missed.

At the 2021 Southern Baptist Convention in Nashville, TN, there was much attention given to topics such as the abolition of abortion, the sin of sexual abuse, the race toward racial reconciliation, and the importance of women's roles in the local church—and rightly so. All of these are necessary and deserving of the utmost attention. Yet, one institution that was given little to no attention is the very one that is the root of all of these issues—the decline and disregard for marriage. I would argue that abortion, sexual abuse, racial reconciliation, and women's roles in the local church are symptoms, not the source. Our neglect for the sanctity of marriage is a slap in the face of God the Father, God the Son, and God the Holy Spirit. The elevation of the institution of marriage to its rightful place in our hearts, homes, churches, and society is the key to moving closer to the abolition of abortion, the abolition of sexual abuse, reconciling racially, and affirming women in the church.

She Says

The trafficking of children has become something I'm very passionate about. It makes me sick that we share a planet with such evil people. It's in every state, every city, and every neighborhood. When I was growing up, we were outside until we heard our parents yell out the front door for us as the sun was setting at night. I'm often envious of my parents. What did they do with all of that free time? We had a community, and everyone's mom and dad was like an extension of my mom and dad. They shared in the responsibility of raising us kids.

But I don't feel the comfort of even letting our girls walk around the neighborhood without each other, a friend, or better yet, the dog. The more I learn about child trafficking, the more I see it all around us. When you go to the mall or library, do you see a creepy guy hanging out by the exit, smoking a cigarette and looking at his phone? Have you ever wondered why he's just hanging out there in the middle of the day with nowhere to go? It's because he is working. He's hunting. He's looking for a young kid who doesn't have anyone paying attention. A kid who needs a savior. He's up to no good.

And it's everywhere.

I LOVE kids. All kids but especially teenagers. I've worked in our church youth group for years and years and sometimes after we meet on Wednesday or Sunday nights, I'll see girls start to walk home. I always go get them and give them a ride, and I tell them to never ever do that. Teenagers just don't have the ability to see the dangers of things like that. Especially teenagers whose parents are too busy to pay attention to what they are doing and to coach them about the evil dangers of it. Or worse, teens who don't have parents at all. We have too many parents who are too busy or AWOL, and it's harming our society.

One evening Sam and I were driving home from a Friday night date and saw 3 girls walking down the street. It was late and cold—in the 40's. This was right outside our quaint, cookie cutter, middle class neighborhood. I heard God tell me to go get those girls off the street. I turned the car around (Sam was following behind me) and pulled over to ask them if they needed a ride somewhere. I saw their relief, and they piled into my car. Immediately they started apologizing about the mud they had all over them. I didn't care about a muddy car. Those girls needed off the street. Long story short, they were the ages of our girls, had run away from foster care, met "a guy" on Instagram, and he was picking them up at the grocery store by our house for the weekend. Um, nope. I later paced the house until 2:00 am when I finally got a call from the police that they had been returned.

This doesn't only happen to runaway orphans. This happens to kids whose parents aren't paying attention. Parents who are working hard to make ends meet. Dads who have checked out of the family due to a porn addiction or another woman at the office. Moms who are bored with the ebb and flow of life and looking for excitement or greener grass. Satan has all kinds of traps. He has us so busy chasing the American dream and keeping up with the Joneses that we are neglecting our God-given roles as parents and spouses. We need to be filling our family's needs so they aren't seeking it somewhere else.

It's easy to let our kids scroll the internet or social media and think they aren't hurting anyone. It's an easy babysitter. But easy usually comes at a high price. It's hurting THEM. Teen girls are comparing themselves to perfectly edited photos on Instagram, and the boys have an unlimited supply of porn. This is shaping them, and we have to stop it. These boys are requesting lewd pictures from our daughters on disappearing apps and sharing them with their friends. These same daughters are so embarrassed they fell for it that they aren't telling their parents driving them further away from the family unit. Those who create these apps aren't stupid. They are targeting our families. Our children. We need to wake up and parent our kids because if we don't, the world will snatch them.

The police told me it would have been years, if ever, before those girls would have been seen again if Sam and I hadn't gotten them off the street. Wow. That was right in my nice, quaint, middle-class neighborhood. It's all around us. And Satan loves it. He loves to devour our kids. He loves to break up marriages. He loves to weaken the family unit God created. He loves how we fight over "choice."

Not only do I love teenagers, but I love having a house full of them. I love community the way I had it growing up. Sam and I decided early on that we wanted to be "that house." The house where all the kids wanted to hang out.

Thankfully, other families entrust us to let their kids sleep over, and we've had a wonderful experience hosting parties and sleepovers and just investing in the next generation. My girls always roll their eyes when we all sit around the bar in the kitchen, and I pass on wisdom to their friends. I pray one day they will look back and see that as serving others. Often, they'll listen to someone else's mom more than their own. I pray for mentors for my girls, too, when I'm not around.

So, I challenge you to take some time investing in the next generation. Grab some teenagers for a Bible study or grab a nearly or newlywed couple and invite them for dinner. I know the task feels overwhelming, like there's too much work, and it'll never be enough. But for that one kid or couple, you can change their life.

We still pray for those three young girls. We don't know what ever happened to them, but I pray that bringing them into our home, giving them some warm, dry socks and a snack and letting them call their families shifted something in their lives. We may never know, but we do know that God calls us to forget our selfish desires, look after the orphans and widows, and serve others. Until this world ends, there will be orphans and widows, and our work will never be done. Let's not be stained by the world but transformed by the power of the Holy Spirit.

And let's not be weary in doing His good work.

xoxo

Me, myself and I are the three biggest threats to marriage.

Marriage Is Not About Me

Me, myself and I are the three biggest threats to marriage. Marriage, the way God intended, has never been and will never be about me, myself, and I. Your marriage is for another, not you. If we want to start making marriage matter, then we must stop elevating self over spouse. The best way to start making marriage matter is to make your marriage matter. You make marriage matter when you make your marriage matter. How do you make your marriage matter?

Serve your spouse. The four Gospels of Matthew, Mark, Luke and John each highlight a different aspect of the Lord Jesus. Matthew portrays Jesus as the Sovereign. Luke portrays Jesus as the Savior. John portrays Jesus as the Son. Mark portrays Jesus as the Servant. In Mark 10:45, the Bible says:

For even the Son of Man came not to be served but to serve, and to give his life as a ransom for many.

What a powerful statement of the reason Christ came!

Don't miss the fact that Jesus came to give, not to take. Obviously, Jesus came to give His life for many people. All people who believe God raised Jesus from the dead and confess that Jesus is Lord will be saved. Yes, Jesus gave His life for MANY, but my prayer is that YOU can say, "Jesus gave His life as a ransom for ME." Can you say that? Do you know that Jesus came to die for you? Have you trusted Him personally as your Savior? You can right now. Stop reading. Start praying. Pray something like this:

> Father, I know that I am a sinner. I know my sin has separated me from You. Also, I know the wages of my sin is death. But, I also know that because You love me, You didn't want to leave me separated from You. You proved Your love for me by sending Jesus to die in my place. The resurrection of Jesus is proof that He alone can forgive me. I am coming to Jesus by faith alone and am ready to follow Him as Lord. Please forgive me. Come into my life. Save me. Thank you!

Please understand that praying certain words doesn't save, but believing the Word does save! Faith doesn't come from speaking certain words, but faith comes from hearing the Word of Christ. Don't pass up this opportunity to become a part of God's family.

How did Jesus give His life as a ransom for many? He chose to serve and not be served. He took the form of a servant in human flesh. He served. What better place to follow the servant leadership of the Lord Jesus than in the marriage relationship? Serve one another as Jesus served us. Husbands and wives, serve one another. Husbands, serve your wife with no expectation that she will serve you back. Wives, serve your husband with no expectation that he will serve you back. Then, you'll never have any unmet expectations or be disappointed in not being served. Go out of your way to serve your spouse.

GOSPEL CONVERSATIONAL MARRIAGE

Think of different ways to serve your spouse. Here are a few:

- Take your wife's car to be detailed.

- Fill up your wife's car with gas.

- Jump up and carry all the groceries in for her.

- Be her biggest cheerleader.

- Don't complain for 24 hours.

- Wink at her from across the room.

- Mop the floor.

- Unload the dishwasher.

- Send your husband a text just to say "Thank you!"

- Put toothpaste on his toothbrush.

- Turn on "your" song and start dancing.

- Give him a back rub.

- Let him sleep in late.

- Compliment him in front of his buddies.

- Initiate sex with him. AMEN!

- When he is sick, wait on him hand and foot.

- Initiate sex with him. Can't be on the list enough!

Surely, you can come up with even more creative ways to serve your spouse.

Pursue your spouse. Do you recall, before you were married, when you were in hot pursuit of your spouse-to-be? Guys, you were pursuing your bride-to-be like Boss Hogg and Rosco P. Coltrane were pursuing Bo and Luke Duke! Ladies, you were pursuing your husband-to-be like Kelly pursued Brandon on 90210!

What happened? Life? School? Kids? Career? The American dream? Why are you pursuing a better life more than you are pursuing your spouse? Why are you pursuing your continued education more than you are pursuing your spouse? Why are you pursuing your kids more than you are pursuing your spouse? Why are you pursuing the American dream more than your spouse? It's time to stop not pursuing your spouse and start pursuing your spouse.

Get to know your spouse even more. Never stop learning about him or her. People change. Keep asking questions to learn more. Spend more time learning what is important to him or her. Ask God to give you the grace to care about what your spouse cares about. Ask. Seek. Knock. Don't stop!

Pay attention to your spouse. Be thoughtful, patient, and kind. Give grace when he or she needs grace. Give encouragement when encouragement is needed. Give an ear when an ear is needed. How are you going to know what he or she needs if you aren't paying attention? Quit playing around, put the PlayStation down, and start paying attention to your spouse!

Flirt with your spouse. So many issues in marriage would be solved if husband and wife spent time flirting with one another. In 2 Timothy 2:22, the Bible says:

GOSPEL CONVERSATIONAL MARRIAGE

So flee youthful passions and pursue righteousness, faith, love, and peace, along with those who call on the Lord with a pure heart.

To flee from youthful passions doesn't mean flirt with youthful passions. God has given us the greatest vehicle to flee from youthful passions—marriage. The best way for a married couple to flee from youthful passions is to flirt with your spouse. You want to flee from sin, flirt with your spouse. Send each other flirtatious tweets. Have fun! Enjoy one another!

Make sacrifices for your spouse. In other words, take something that is valuable to you—time, money, interests, preferences—and give it up for your spouse who is even *more valuable*. When you make such a sacrifice it tells your spouse that she or he means more to you than literally anything on this planet. Does he mean more to you than shopping at your favorite store? Show him! Does she mean more to you than sitting in your favorite deer stand? Show her!

Date your spouse. After twenty years of marriage, I can't begin to tell you how fun it is to date Tonya. It gets more fun each year. Friday night is date night and our church knows it, our kids know it, and our friends know it. Nothing competes with date night. Nothing. Date night might be a dinner out, a movie at the theater, or a lazy night at home, but it is always Tonya and me. Go ahead and try to schedule something with Tonya and Sam Greer on a Friday night, and you will be disappointed!

Plan a getaway. Sit down together and plan a getaway for just the two of you. There are three types of trips your family should plan throughout the year: Presbyterian trip, Baptist trip, and Pentecostal trip.

The Presbyterian trip involves the whole family and is ALL PRE-PLANNED. Every detail. Every excursion. Every meal. Every day of the trip is pre-planned.

The Baptist trip is a bit more loosely planned. Yes, kids are welcome to come on this trip as well. Sure, you know where you are going, you know you are going to eat like a Baptist, but you still have free will to choose to change the plan at any moment.

The Pentecostal trip is for mom and dad only. Kids are not allowed on this trip. No exceptions. Why? Because much of this trip involves speaking in tongues and the laying on of hands! The Pentecostal trip is not child friendly. Plan a Pentecostal getaway with your spouse.

Forgive your spouse. No, I didn't save the easiest one for last. Forgiving is tough. Forgiving can be rough. And on top of that, we can't ever forgive enough. In Matthew 18:21-22, Jesus was asked about forgiveness:

> *Then Peter came up and said to him, "Lord, how often will my brother sin against me, and I forgive him? As many as seven times?" Jesus said to him, "I do not say to you seven times, but seventy-seven times."*

Peter was looking for a limit to forgiveness. Jesus said forgiveness is limitless. Seventy times seven is four-hundred and ninety! Can you think of any scenario whereby you would even be given the opportunity to forgive someone four-hundred and ninety times? Johnny Hunt said:

> When would we ever forgive someone that many times. Get married and you'll know! Forgiving that many times becomes a habit. What would happen if forgiveness became our habit in marriage.[xxi]

The forgiven must forgive. What better place to showcase forgiveness than in marriage! Forgiveness is endless. Forgiveness was given to you to be given to another. Don't just get forgiveness, give it! Start with your spouse. Pray that God will grant you the grace to forgive. Forgive her. Forgive him. As P.S. Walker has said:

> Whenever my wife apologizes first, after a fight, I feel like I lost.

Even if you lose the fight, you can still win. Be the first to forgive. Forgive her first. Forgive him first. Look at one another with the same grace and mercy like you used to look at each other.

CONVERSATION STARTERS

1. What does it mean that marriage is to be held in honor among all? Discuss.

2. What are some of your favorite marriage moments? Discuss as a couple.

3. Make a list of ways you can serve your spouse each week. Give up something of value once per month to show your spouse that he or she is more valuable.

4. Discuss forgiveness. Talk through areas in your marriage that you have yet to forgive one another.

SAM & TONYA GREER

Conversation 5

Marriage and Money

Keep your life free from love of money, and be content with what you have, for he has said, "I will never leave you nor forsake you."
Hebrews 13:5

How does God view money? How should money be viewed in the marriage relationship? Why do most conversations about money in marriage end in a fight? How can a husband and wife establish a realistic budget? What does life after debt look like?

Render to Little Caesar's What is Little Caesar's

The more I asked the more I heard, "Don't do it! It will decrease the value of your home. Don't do it! It is too much to keep up. Don't do it! It will make it difficult to sell your house." Don't' do it. Don't do it. Don't do it. Well, we did it, and we would do it again and again and again. We put an inground pool in our backyard.

Initially, we viewed it as a family investment not a financial investment. Tonya and I decided that we wanted to be the house where all Braydee and Belle's friends gather. Guess what? We are that house! I am sure the reason why middle schoolers and high schoolers want to be at our house is because Tonya and I are so cool. Surely it has nothing to do with having a pool, right? God has allowed us to use the pool as a way to build relationships with unchurched students and families. Not to mention, my girls love laying out and getting in the pool as well!

We've had birthday parties, end of school parties where Braydee and Belle's whole class attended, church gatherings, cookouts, hang outs, and layouts all at our pool. What do you do when twenty middle schoolers have a summer night party at your pool and they get hungry? You make a pizza run to Little Caesar's, and you render to Little Caesar's what is Little Caesar's. Does it cost money to put in a pool? Yes. Does it cost money to maintain a pool? Yes. Does it cost money to feed every middle schooler and high schooler in Hamilton County who attend parties at your pool? Yes. Is it worth it? Absolutely. Our pool has been a strong family and kingdom investment.

Tonya and I prepared ourselves for a decrease in the value of our home after putting in the pool. Then, about three years after installing our inground pool, the coronavirus went viral. As a result, inground swimming pools became a hot ticket item in a quarantined world. What we paid to install an inground pool doubled after COVID-19. Our house value skyrocketed due in part because we put in a pool. Let me be clear, we are not savvy financial investors. We installed a pool solely as an investment in our family, not a financial one. Yet, God blessed. When you use money for investing in others, God will bless you. When you use money in your marriage to invest in others, God will bless you and your marriage.

In marriage, it's not easy marrying marriage and money, but marrying marriage and money is what we must do. Many questions abound when it comes to marriage and money. Whose money is it? How does God view money? How should money be viewed in marriage? How important is a budget? How do you make a budget?

These questions and more beg the question: where do we start when it comes to marriage and money? We must start with our hearts.

It Ain't Nothing 'Til I Call It

"Stee-rike three! [insert arm motions] You're out!" Bill Klem, the father of baseball umpires, was the first umpire to use arm signals while working behind the plate. Klem umped for thirty-seven years, including eighteen World Series. On one occasion, while he was behind the plate, the pitcher pitched, the catcher caught, and the batter didn't swing. For a second or two, Klem said nothing.

The batter blurted out, "Okay, so what was it, a ball or a strike?"

Klem responded, "Sonny, it ain't nothing 'til I call it."

The baseball diamond is ruled by the umpire. The players play. The managers manage. The coaches coach. The fans cheer. But the umpire rules the diamond. Sure, the managers, players, fans, and coaches can complain, but the umpire's word is the only one that matters. He rules.

In any relationship, someone has to call the shots. Even if the other folks involved don't like it someone has the last word. One college baseball manager and the umpire were going at it on the field when the umpire yelled at the manager,

"Go where I can't see you anymore!"

So, the manager went and stood over home plate.

Ouch! From shouting matches between managers and umpires to shen-anigans by both umpires and managers, the umpire still rules the diamond.

For far too many people the almighty dollar, not the Almighty God, is ruling in their hearts.

We know who rules the baseball diamond, but who rules the human heart? Who sits on the throne of the human heart? Who rules your heart? In Colossians 3:15, the Bible says:

And let the peace of Christ rule in your hearts...

The word "rule" comes from the Greek word *brabeuo* which means "rule," "control," "acts as judge," "act as umpire."[xxii] Let the peace of Christ umpire your life. Let the peace of Christ call the shots in your life. Let the peace of Christ have the last word in your life. For far too many people the almighty dollar, not the Almighty God, is ruling in their hearts. Let the Almighty God rule your almighty dollars so the almighty dollar won't rule you.

The Almighty God's View of the Almighty Dollar

How does the Almighty God view the almighty dollar? God's Word doesn't change when it comes to the subject of the smallest of change. The Bible is not neutral when it comes to the largest of bills. The Scriptures make sense when it comes to dollars and cents. God's Word isn't silent when it comes to the subject of "ching ching." Jesus talked much about money. Sixteen of the thirty-seven parables are concerned with how to handle money and possessions. In the Gospels, one out of ten verses deal directly with money. The Scriptures offer over 500 verses on prayer, less than 500 verses on faith, but more than 2,000 verses on money and possessions.

Why so many verses on money? Now, it is true that not all of the verses that contain the mention of money are teaching how to handle money. In fact, Jesus would often use money to teach different spiritual principles because money is something universally known. Yet, God clearly lays out in Scripture His view of money. Consider at least three different Scriptures whereby God's Word warns against the love of money.

First, contemplate Paul's warning to Timothy in 1 Timothy 6:10:

For the love of money is a root of all kinds of evils.

Why are you mad at money? Money ain't done nothing to you! Money is not a root of all kinds of evils. The *love of money* is a root of all kinds of evils. Just like guns are not the problem when it comes to gun violence. Guns don't cause gun violence; people do! Similarly, money is not the problem when it comes to money problems. Money is not your problem. You are your problem. Your first love is not God, not your spouse, not your family, not your church, not your neighbor, but your first love is money. You are all about them Benjamins, that paper, and making a buck! Your first thought with every decision you make is not, "What would God have me do? What do you think honey? How will this affect the people in my life?" Rather, your first and foremost thought is, "How much will it cost? How much can I make?" It is time for you to repent!

Attention: you will not be the first person in human history to master being mastered by both God and money!

Second, consider what Jesus said about money in Matthew 6:24:

No one can serve two masters, for either he will hate the one and love the other, or he will be devoted to the one and despise the other. You cannot serve God and money.

I know you think you are something else. Don't we all? Attention: you will not be the first person in human history to master being mastered by both God and money! No one will ever be able to serve two masters. No one. Not even you. You are either serving the Almighty God, or you are serving the almighty dollar. You are not serving both and you never will. Why? You can't.

Money may be the master of many people's universe, but don't allow money to master you. Dr. Albert Mohler shared the following two gospel conversation starter questions that he often asks: (1) What do you do for a living? (2) What are you living for? People enjoy talking about themselves and what they do for a living; however, people rarely even think about what they are living for. Americans are taught from an early age to finish school in order to find a good career in order to live the American dream. Of course, the American dream is fueled by the almighty dollar. Jesus came teaching about the kingdom of God, not the American dream. Jesus is the Almighty God come to teach about using the almighty dollar and not allowing oneself to be used by it.

God knows we can't erase the ongoing need for money, but He also knows we must escape the ongoing want for more money.

Third, examine the author of Hebrews words concerning the love of money in Hebrews 13:5:

Keep your life free from love of money.

God never expects us to be free from fees. Furthermore, fees are not free. God is not instructing us to be free from money. He is commanding us to be free from the love of money, free from the devotion to money, free from being mastered by money, and free from living for money. Notice how Hebrews 13:5 follows the very passage whereby the author addressed marriage being held in honor among all and the purity of the marriage bed. Is it a coincidence that the love of money comes right after love and marriage in Hebrews? No, not a coincidence, but providence. God knows that we can't erase the ongoing need for money, but He also knows we must escape the ongoing want for more money.

God views money as something we need, but He also views money as something we want more than we need.

What is the answer to the question of how God views money? What is the Almighty God's view of the almighty dollar? What is the bottom line? God views money as something we need, but He also views money as something we want more than we need. Stated simply: Money is needed, but it shouldn't be wanted more than it is needed. Our problem is that we want money much more than we need it, and we need God much more than we want Him. God help us! God have mercy on us!

Somebody Stole Our Tent

Dad joke alert! I need to be like a comedian at a building construction conference—*I gotta level with you.* I gotta shoot straight with you. The Greer family's idea of camping is staying in a hotel. We would love to love camping, but we don't even like camping. We tried it. It was fine. Well, it was fine for the first day. It was not-so-okay the second day. By the third day, we were hoping for a miracle. You know the third day is when what is dead comes to life. Amen! Even on the third day camping was dead to us. Camping is still not resurrected in our hearts. I have heard others who love camping speak of the warmth of the campfire, the allure of the outdoors, and the view of the stars.

Sherlock Holmes and Dr. Watson pitched their camping tent under the stars and fell asleep. Sometime in the middle of the night, Holmes wakes Watson:

"Watson, look up at the stars and tell me what you deduce."

Watson says: "I see millions of stars, and if even a few of those have planets, it's quite likely there are some planets like Earth, and if there are a few planets like Earth out there, there might also be life."

Holmes replies, "Watson, you idiot, somebody stole our tent!"[xxiii]

Pack it up. Pack it in. Please let it end.

Three days into our camping excursion and we were hoping the game would be afoot and someone would steal our tent. We were done. No one in our family was even pretending anymore to be the outdoorsy type. As we were packing up, I had the tune of "Jump Around" from the band *House of Pain* playing in my head with some edited lyrics: "Pack it up. Pack it in. Please let it end." Like it or not, all believers are spending a lifetime camping in earthly tents until Jesus comes again or He calls us home.

In 2 Corinthians 5:1-4, Paul the apostle wrote about the human body being an earthly tent:

For we know that if the tent that is our earthly home is destroyed, we have a building from God, a house not made with hands, eternal in the heavens. For in this tent we groan, longing to put on our heavenly dwelling, if indeed by putting it on we may not be found naked. For while we are still in this tent, we groan, being burdened—not that we would be unclothed, but that we would be further clothed, so that what is mortal may be swallowed up by life.

The apostle Paul pointed out that for believers the flesh is temporary housing for our souls. He says that we groan while in this earthly tent because we are burdened to get home to heaven. Paul David Tripp humorously but accurately illustrates this present groaning and longing for our future home while in these earthly tents.

> Most of us have no pilgrim experience, so perhaps the closest thing in our experience to the journey of a pilgrim is rustic camping. I am persuaded that the whole purpose of camping is to make a person long for home! On that first day in the woods, putting up the tent is exciting, but three days later your tent has unpleasant odors you can't explain. You love the taste of food cooked over an open flame (that's ash!), but three days later you are tired of foraging for wood and irritated by how fast it burns. You were excited at the prospect of catching your dinner from the stream running past your campsite, which is reported to be teeming with trout, but all you have snagged are the roots on the bottom.
>
> You're now four days in and your back hurts, there seems to be no more felled wood to forage, and you're tired of keeping the fire going anyway.
>
> You look into what was once an ice-and-food-filled cooler to see the family-sized steaks you have reserved floating gray and oozing in a pool of blood-stained water. Suddenly you begin to think fondly of home .... You stand there hoping that someone will break the silence and say, "Why don't we go home?" Your four days in the wilderness have accomplished their mission. They have prepared you to appreciate home! Our world isn't a very good amusement park. No, it's a broken place groaning for

redemption. Here is meant to make us long for forever. Here is meant to prepare us for eternity.[xxiv]

What a strong reminder that believers are pilgrims on this planet, wanderers in this world, elect exiles on this earth, aliens in America, and hikers on our way home to heaven.

Living in the Tent of Contentment

So many tents. Big tents. Small tents. Pricey tents. Affordable tents. Easy to put up tents. Impossible to put up tents. Too many tents. Finding just the right tent can add a certain amount of anxiety to an already anxious outing. Fortunately, when it comes to these earthly tents we walk around in every day, there are only two from which to choose: (1) the tent of con*tent*ment and (2) the tent of discon*tent*ment. Paul wrote in 1 Timothy 6:6-8:

Now there is great gain in godliness with contentment, for we brought nothing into the world, and we cannot take anything out of the world. But if we have food and clothing, with these we will be content.

What does Paul mean that there is *great gain in godliness with contentment*? When we learn how to be content in any and all situations, then we will grow in godliness. When we learn that our satisfaction is found in the Creator and not in His creation, we will grow in godliness. When we learn that we are to love the Lord Jesus more than our ministry, then we will grow in godliness. When we learn that we are to love God the giver more than what He gives, we will grow in godliness. Have you learned how to be content with little or much? Have you learned how to possess your possessions and not allow your possessions to possess you?

Living in the tent of contentment means leaving the tent of discontentment.

Choose today to be content. Be content with your home. Be content with your career. Be content in your marriage. Does that mean you are settling? No. Does it mean that you can't work toward improvement? No, it means you are being faithful with what God has provided. Be content with what you have and stop coveting what you don't have. Be thankful for what you have and stop being thoughtful of what you don't have. Living in the tent of contentment means leaving the tent of discontentment.

Leaving the Tent of Discontentment

Some of you, thus far, have staked your life in the tent of discontentment. What was meant by Paul's words *we brought nothing into the world, and we cannot take anything out of the world*? Naked we entered the world and naked we will exit the world. We started with nothing and we will end with nothing. From an earthly perspective, we are nothing to nothing. If that be the case, then why do we spend our time, resources, money, talents, gifts, education, and experience chasing after somethings. Life is not found in the somethings, but life is found in someone—Jesus!

Jesus was the most content person to ever walk planet earth. What did he have? He had nothing and at the same time He had everything. The One who left the glory of heaven had nowhere to lay His head on earth. Yet, that same One, by whom all authority in heaven and on earth had been given, was now here. From man's perspective, Jesus had nothing. From heaven's perspective, He had everything. Do you realize that if you are in Christ you are a co-heir with the Lord Jesus? You may not have much here on earth and when you die you will take nothing with you from earth. Or, you may have much on earth and when you die you will still take nothing with you from earth. If you are in Christ, you have an inheritance kept in heaven for you. Oh my soul!

In light of this truth, why are you chasing after the monster of more? Why are you giving into the green-eyed monster of greed? Why are you consumed with consumerism? Being consumed with consumerism is anti-gospel. Taking rather than giving is anti-gospel. Having and not helping is anti-gospel. Leave the lifestyle of chasing after somethings, and live in the life of the someone. Rest in Jesus. Trust in Jesus. Don't fall into the trap of what Paul David Tripp said is the "If only I had this, then I would be" deception. Tripp added:

> Whatever sits on the other side of your "if only" is one of the places you are looking for life. If only I had this job, if only I had this house, if only I had this relationship, if only I had this experience, if only, if only, if only, if only. It's a heart that's still looking for life. What a tragedy when you've been given life and you are still looking for life! What a tragedy if you're looking horizontally for what you've already been given vertically! There are hundreds of thousands of believers who've been given life who are still searching for life. What a tragedy![xxv]

Whose Money Is It Anyway?

Early on in ministry my mentor and pastor, Dr. Chuck Herring, warned against the two pitfalls whereby ministers are most likely to experience a moral failure. Being alone with a person of the opposite sex who is not one's spouse and having no accountability in place to guard against the misuse and abuse of money. I established a policy early on never to be alone with a woman who is not Tonya. Also, I have been careful to operate with much financial accountability. Meanwhile, God has such a sense of humor. I have prayed for years for God to protect me from the potential pitfalls involving women and money. God, then, gave me three women—Braydee, Belle, and Tonya. They ensure that money always stays away from me!

Is it yours? Is it hers? Is it his? Is it mine? Is it theirs? Does it belong to them? Whose money is it anyway? In Deuteronomy 10:14, the Bible says:

Behold, to the LORD your God belong heaven and the heaven of heavens, the earth with all that is in it.

In whatever language you speak, the word "all" always means "all." The almighty dollar is included in *the earth and all that is in it*. Your money is not yours, not hers, and not his. All money belongs to the LORD your God. The only percentage of money that belongs to God is 100%; therefore, the percentage of money that belongs to you is 0%. Please don't think for one minute that you get to decide what percentage of "your" money belongs to God.

Think about the most expensive thing you have ever purchased. Maybe a phone? Maybe a laptop? Maybe a pool? Maybe a car? Maybe a house? Do you have it in mind? What is the most expensive thing you have ever bought? We could total the most expensive purchases throughout all of human history and they wouldn't come close to the most expensive purchase God made. In fact, God's purchase was so expensive that He alluded to it in an unforgettable way. In Mark 8:36, Mark wrote:

For what does it profit a man to gain the whole world and forfeit his soul?

God purchased the souls of men, women, boys and girls with the precious blood of Jesus. Jesus' blood is more precious than gold. You were bought at a very expensive price. Jesus paid the whole price for your sin and mine.

Salvation belongs to our God. Money belongs to our God. Gold belongs to our God. The heavens and the earth belong to our God. You belong to our God. Stop kidding yourself. You're not doing God a favor by giving Him a percentage of what He already owns anyway.

When you buy into the fact that all money belongs to God, it will change everything about how you spend, save and give. Your financial goals will change. Your budget will change. The way you think about money will change. The way you talk about money will change.

One Bank Account, Not Two

God doesn't expect us to understand all that He is doing, but He does expect us to stand under all that He is doing. At the same time, God does expect us to under-stand some of what He is doing. He expects us to under-stand the design of marriage between one husband and one wife. God designed marriage for a husband and wife to become one flesh. The two become one.

How can the two become one flesh when you have his and her bank accounts? His and her bank accounts add up to two not one. Yes, his and her deodorant is fine. His and her shampoo is fine. His and her toothbrushes are fine. His and her closets are fine. His and her bank accounts are not fine. Why? Because where your treasure is there your heart will be also. To truly give your spouse your heart, you must give up "your" account. Decide right now to *merge your money*. Seriously, stop trying to operate with separate his and her bank accounts. Please know that operating with a joint bank account is essential in marriage. Yes, husband and wife, you heard it here. Operating with a joint bank account is essential in marrying marriage and money.

Art Rainer offers some sound reasons why married couples should have a joint bank account or joint bank accounts. When you have joint accounts, you are holding one another accountable in your spending. When you have joint accounts, you are teaming up to tackle all expenditures. When you have joint accounts, you are trusting one another with finances. When you have joint accounts, you are not spending in secret.[xxvi]

Slide ya boy some dough!

Rainer makes a strong case for married couples having a joint bank account or accounts. I would add that when you have joint accounts in marriage, it fosters more conversations about money, not less. Husbands and wives, we need to be talking more about money. Money conversations don't have to end in a fight. I know they often do, but they don't have to. Here's a recent example.

One of our church students texted his mom, "Slide ya boy some dough!" I assume that means give me some money, please. Well, maybe give me some money without the *please*. I probably shouldn't make you aware of this, but I am anyway. Like this student, I like to carry cash. I am a cash guy. I don't like plastic. I don't like debit/credit cards. I like those dollar, dollar bills y'all! Why? When you take cash out of your wallet and pay for something, that cash will never go back into your wallet. Never. You actually can see, touch and feel the money leaving your wallet. On the contrary, when you take out that debit/credit card and swipe it you put it right back in your wallet. You feel no tangible loss. Your wallet has lost nothing. Five minutes later you can swipe again. I am convinced that you count the cost more when you use cash and not cards.

It drives Tonya NUTS when she pulls out the debit card in a restaurant and I ask her,

"Is there enough money in the account to pay for this meal? If not, I can pay in cash."

Nothing gets under Tonya's skin more. She NEVER likes for me to ask such questions in public. To her credit 99.999% of the time there is plenty of money in the account, which is no surprise as Tonya keeps track of every penny that comes in and out. In a recent outing, I asked her if there was enough money in the account to pay for the meal, and she got fired up! I guess after twenty years of asking this question in public I should start asking her in private. In an *I-am-tired-of-you-asking-me-this-in-public* heated and spirited kind of way, Tonya assured me that there was enough. She was ready to let me have it, when it happened. Our server returned and said,

"I am sorry. Your card was declined. Do you have another card you would like for me to run?"

That conversation about money could have turned into a fight quickly, but Tonya and I couldn't help but laugh at the irony of the situation. It was quite hilarious. And I have never been so thankful for a declined card.

Don't hoard "your" money, hide "your" money, or hope in "your" money; rather, hold loosely to "your" money and tightly to your honey!

Conversations about money don't have to be fights between husband and wife. Merging "your" money is a great place to start having more of a gospel conversational marriage. What does it profit a man to bow his knee to money and forfeit his vows to his honey? Husbands and wives, don't bow your knee to "your" money and neglect your vows to your honey. Don't hoard "your" money, hide "your" money, or hope in "your" money; rather, hold loosely to "your" money and tightly to your honey! Merge "your" money! Despite the reports that fighting over money is the second leading cause of divorce, married couples can fight back by eliminating debt, building a practical budget, and having more conversations about money.[xxvii]

Build a Basic Budget

By building a basic budget, you are giving your money a place to go. If you don't give your money a place to go, then it will be gone! If you don't give your money a place to go, then it will be like the gas in Tonya's car, gone! If you don't give your money a place to go, then it will be like the milk in the empty milk carton in the fridge, gone! If you don't give your money a place to go, then it will be like Dr. Gregg Hauss' hair on his head, gone! If you don't give your money a place to go, then it will be like the first fifty years of Melissa Atchley's life, gone! Build a budget.

Do you have a budget? Do you have a real budget? Do you have a realistic budget? Are you and your spouse on the same page when it comes to your budget? Let's find out. Grab your favorite caffeine beverage, a computer, and don't forget your spouse. Start a basic budget building conversation right now.

If your money has nowhere to go, then it will be gone!

Know what is coming in. What is your monthly income? What are you and your spouse bringing in every month? Take a moment and add up the money you bring home after taxes and deductions. Also, add in any additional sources of monthly income. Remember, building a basic budget is not a one-time marriage experience, but it's a lifetime exercise. As you continue to work, your pay will likely increase. As you add more people to your home, your expenses will definitely increase.

Get this! Tonya just sent me a text about more stimulus money that is being sent to Americans. I am serious. She just now at 12:32 p.m. on Tuesday, July 13, 2021 sent me a pic of a letter from The White House regarding the child tax relief payment. This is a real time example of the changing nature of budgets. Make sure you pay attention to what is coming in every month and review your budget at least once per year.

Know what is going out. A healthy budget should reflect income and outflow. Make an honest list of your expenses. Start with categories such as housing, food, internet, phone, power, etc. Don't forget to add the expense of the fourteen different streaming services to which you subscribe while at the same time you still have to purchase movies that are not included with your streaming subscriptions. Sorry, I am just ranting a bit about subscriptions. We have more subscriptions than our local CVS issues prescriptions.

Take the time to calculate actual numbers for the different categories of monthly expenses. For any bill you pay quarterly or annually, figure out what the cost is monthly and include that expense in your monthly budget. The purpose of a budget is not to remind you of what you are saying "no" to, but to allow you to know what you can start saying "yes" to.

Knock out debt. We know there is life after death. Jesus told us in Revelation 1:18:

I died, and behold I am alive forevermore, and I have the keys of Death and Hades.

Everyone is looking for someone who has been to the other side and back. What is on the other side of death? Is there life? Jesus has died, returned from the dead, and He is alive forevermore. For all who are in Christ, there is not only life before death but there is life after death. What's more, Jesus promised there is life after death forevermore. Life without end. Life eternal. Not just life for a time, or for a season, or for a little while, or for a minute, or for a lifetime, but life forevermore.

While we are still living in this life before death, is there life after debt? Is it possible to experience life after debt? One of my friends, who is thirty-seven years old, just paid off his house. He literally has no debt whatsoever. Wow! How do we move toward experiencing life after debt? Pay off debt! Start by knocking out the small debt first. By using this snowball approach of paying off debt balances, you will gain confidence along the way. Celebrate paying off the smallest of debts and then start attacking larger debt. Do away with debt! You can do this!

Why is it vitally important that married couples work hard to experience life after debt? Is this even a problem? Most marriages start off in debt. In fact, nearly two-thirds of all marriages start off in debt. The debt pandemic among marrieds continues to grow at a rapid pace. Twice the number of couples today, 85%, start off in debt compared to 43% of couples who were married just twenty-five years ago and began in debt. Meanwhile, 94% of people who say they have a "great" marriage discuss their money dreams with their spouse.[xxviii] Keep talking about money. Have more conversations about money. Talk about how to knock out debt.

You can either give money, spend money, save money, or invest money.

Know what is being put back. You can either give money, spend money, save money, or invest money. Do you know what you are giving? Do you know what you are spending? Do you know what you are saving? Do you know what you are investing? What is your plan when your plan falls apart? Do you have a nest egg tucked away for a rainy day? Are you contributing to your retirement? What would you like to accomplish through your saving and/or investing? What are your financial goals? What type of income would you like to live on when you retire? What will it take to save for college or an upcoming wedding? Or, if you are like me, what will it take to save for two upcoming weddings?

Set back some cash for life's setbacks. Life happens. Does your savings account reflect the reality that you are expecting the unexpected to happen? A good place to start is put back $1,000 to $2,000 for deductibles of unexpected car repairs, house repairs, or medical expenses. Also, save three to six months of living expenses. You never know when you will be laid off or let go. Dedicate 10% to

15% of your gross income to your retirement. Work to pay off your mortgage. Save for your child's college or future wedding. Be sure you know what is being put back, and talk about it. One of the best ways to avoid credit cards and protect your ability to be generous is to set back some cash for life's setbacks. Make a plan, so that life's setbacks won't set you back. See a sample of a basic budget at the end of this chapter.

Who is the spender in your marriage? Who is the saver in your marriage? Are both you and your spouse savers? Are y'all both spenders? It is important to know the answers to these questions. Discuss with one another and think about how you can negotiate in your spending and saving. Come to an understanding about how and what you will spend and save.

Tonya rounds down and I round up.

Tonya is a professional spender. She has mastered the art of shopping using round numbers. When Tonya sees a price of $9.99 or $199.00, she rounds the number down. Tonya has said,

"Sam, this is only one hundred dollars."

I reply with,

"Wow! That's a great price."

The lady behind the register rings up the item and says:

"That will be $209.54"

What! I thought it was $100 dollars. Well the price was actually $199.00. Tonya rounds down. I don't do much better when it comes to savings as I round up. For example, $2,700 in savings in my mind is the same as $3,000. How do we reconcile one of us rounding up and the other rounding down? Over the years, we have balanced one another out. I am still the saver, and Tonya is still the spender; but she has become more of a saver, and I have become more of a spender.

Don't Forget About Life Insurance

What if I told you that a maximum $10,000 investment would guarantee a tax-free return of $1,000,000.00, would you be interested? Of course there is one minor catch. You would have to die within the next twenty years. Very few, if any, vehicles offer such a tax-free return like that of a term life insurance policy. But, again, the policy holder must die for the return to be realized.

Statistically, one out of one hundred (1%) term life insurance policy holders die while the policy is in place. My dad was one of the 1%. He died at the age of 32. Husbands and wives, don't forget about life insurance.

Be a Generous Giver

As it relates to giving, tithing is where we start. *Teething* may be a bad word to young parents whose child won't stop screaming; however, *tithing* is not a bad word. "Tithing? But pastor I thought that because we now live in the age of grace we are no longer required to tithe. We are now free from the law and tithing, right?" Technically, we are no longer bound to the tithe, but now we are free to give more than the tithe. We are required to give according to grace, not according to the law. The law says give enough to get by. Grace says I get to give above and beyond. The law says bring 10% of your income to the house of the Lord. Grace says start at 10% but give over and above to Jesus' church and His work to take the gospel to the ends of the earth. The tithe, or 10%, is where we start, not where we stop. The age of the law was the age of just getting by, but the age of grace is the age of generosity.

Imagine two people with the same amount of money and one gave 10% to Jesus and His kingdom while the other gave 0%. One person kept 90% after giving the tithe, while the other person kept 100%. Which person do you believe has more? The person with 90%, who gives to the Lord and His kingdom, always has much more than the person with 100%. I'd much rather live with 90% and God's blessing than live with 100% without His blessing. Don't be mistaken, if you refuse to tithe, then you are stealing. What's more, you're stealing from God. Good luck with that!

What you give away never goes away!

Married couples, tithing is where we start, not where we stop. You know what that means. Some of y'all, who are giving below 10%, haven't even gotten started yet. Let me encourage to bump your giving to the next level. Are you giving no percent? Give 1-5%. Are you giving 1-5%? Give 5-10%. Are you giving 5-10%? Give 10-15%. If you haven't started giving, then start! If you have started giving, then increase your giving and don't stop! What you give away never goes away. More specifically, what you give away to the Lord and His church never goes away!

Give something away daily. How can you begin to cultivate a culture of giving in your heart and home? Steve Gaines shared that one of his goals is to give something away every day. He seeks to practice generosity daily.[xxix]

We are most like God when we give. Our God is a giving God. Let's seek to give something away each day and it will help us cultivate a culture of giving in our hearts and homes. By the way, what you give away doesn't always have to be money. To cultivate a culture of giving, get creative with what you give away. We can give away our place in line, a prayer, a compliment, a word of encouragement, a Scripture verse, a testimony, the gospel, or anything else the Holy Spirit gives you to give away. You were given by God what you were given for one reason: so you could give it away.

Simply ask the Holy Spirit, "What would You have me give away today?" Remember, what you give away for the Lord and His church never goes away! God will use it now and for eternity. As a pastor, I have tried to teach our church staff the importance of what the Bible says in Acts 20:35:

It is more blessed to give than to receive.

Each time we go out for a staff lunch, I remind them that based upon Acts 20:35, they will be blessed if they pay for my lunch. So far, they have all forfeited that blessing. Let's seek to give something away daily.

When you eat out, don't base the percentage of your tip on what your server didn't do, but base it on what your Savior did.

Generosity can point people to Jesus. A church member who opened his own store once told me:

"Pastor, as soon as God blesses me in this business I will give to the church. I want to be able to be generous. As soon as I make it rich, I will be generous."

Wrong. Being rich doesn't make you generous and being poor doesn't keep you from being generous. Being rich and not being poor doesn't make you generous. Being generous makes you generous. The widow with two mites was far more generous than anyone Jesus had ever seen in Israel. She gave not from the overflow. She gave all she had. She held nothing back. What a picture of generosity!

God can use your generosity to point people to Jesus. When you eat out, don't base the percentage of your tip on what your server didn't do, but base it on what your Savior did. Be generous. When you have the opportunity to pay someone else's bill, don't do so based on whether or not they are a good friend, but do so based on the fact that when you were an enemy of God Christ paid your debt in full. Be generous. When you have the opportunity to give, don't do so based on what you will get in return, but do so based on the fact that Jesus will get all the glory. Be generous. Husband and wife, be generous together.

She Says

Sam was long winded on that chapter so I'm gonna wrap this up quickly.

As I said earlier, my parents were divorced, and Sam lost his dad pretty early. So, neither of us knew much about marriage when we got married. I tried to wiggle out of it as long as I could, but he finally nailed a date down and off we went. I wish I could say I was one of those girls excited to get married, that had planned the event from start to finish, knew what dress I wanted and had a church and pastor picked out. But honestly, the only thing I cared about was that we'd have a house close to my parents. I needed them. Sam, bless his heart, has never been a handy man. What if something broke, who would fix it? Who would cut our grass? My dad. That's who. And I liked to shop with my mom on Thursday afternoons. She would buy all our knickknacks for the new house and she's just plain fun. I've always loved being with my mom. We had to stay close.

So, we eloped and bought a house smack in between my parents. My dad cut our grass and fixed stuff while my mom and I shopped, and I went to her house as much as possible.

And yes, we had separate checking accounts. For a WHILE. I couldn't decide which job I wanted to take so I took them both. I really liked money. Sam could pay the house and our cars with "his" money and I'd pay utilities and do the shopping with "my" money. Thankfully, God sent us some really good mentors early in our marriage. Our house right in between my parents also had a church at the back of the neighborhood. After visiting the first Sunday, we knew that was our home. Mark and Peggy Hayman saw us and invited us to their Sunday school class. As I look back on those early years, I realize just how much those two spoke into our lives. We started getting active in their class. Every week was something brand new for us. And best of all, we got a first-hand peek at what a real marriage should look like. Those two had teenagers and had been married for more than half our young lives, and they were just as giddy with each other as two teens in a brand-new love. He adored her and she adored him. They talked often about how his job in life was looking after her needs and her job was looking after his needs. Wow. They talked about how he'd never even raised his voice at her. They were so authentic.

Then they got on my toes. One Sunday they talked about money. He'd brought up separate checking accounts. And leaving and cleaving. And how leaning on your parents too much could be damaging to your marriage.

What? Huh-uh. I like my parents.

Then it got even worse. He talked about how parents giving their grown kids money also gives them power and control in your marriage. Ouch. My momma liked to take me shopping on Thursdays, and I liked my momma taking me shopping on Thursdays. Occasionally she'd throw in a car payment to lighten the load. So, I inquired more and tried to plead. Mark Hayman was FIRM. Cut. It. Out. Leave and cleave.

Ouch. I look back and I don't think I would have done it. We did start tithing early on—me from "my" account and Sam from "his." But then it happened. God forced our hands. Within two years of getting married and joining that church which we came to LOVE, God uprooted us, and moved us to south Louisiana. God called Sam to go to seminary. Let me be clear that I didn't even know what seminary was. I never felt "the call." I did NOT want to do it. I resisted. I stayed behind to "work" while Sam moved without me. God was extremely patient with me. But finally, He said, "GO!" So, I went. I quit my jobs and finally grew up. I went from two jobs to zero, Sam had no job, and momentarily we had rent on an apartment in Louisiana AND a mortgage on a house in Mississippi that hadn't sold. I still have no idea how we pulled that off. But we followed God and He provided everything we needed.

Eventually I did find a job, and within weeks a little church in the middle of nowhere, Bonner Creek Baptist, called Sam to be their pastor. So, we finally did it. We became grownups. We got a joint checking account. But it didn't matter much. After we tithed and paid bills, there was nothing left over. There was nothing to fight about because there was nothing left. For a long time I wondered why so many people fought about money. Now I realized it was because they actually had money! But we were finally all on our own, empty checking account and all!

Don't get me wrong, my mom (and Sam's mom) still like to treat us. They do nice things for special occasions and love to spoil the kids when they can. I even had a deal with my mom long ago. She'd keep them in nice clothes if I'd give her grandchildren. She has more than kept up her end of the bargain. But as far as having parents paying their adult kids' bills, I concur. Cut. It. Out.

In marriage, there's so much that you can negotiate. There's no set rule for how you have to do every single thing. Or spend every penny. As a couple, you work it out. You figure out what works for you.

GOSPEL CONVERSATIONAL MARRIAGE

You give and you take. You can do that with your extra money. Work out what gets you to your goals. It's different for everyone. Our goal is always to tithe first. Then Sam goes to the bank on pay day and takes out his cash, and moves what we agreed to save to the savings account (before I blow it). Then I pay the bills and get what we need. IF anything is left, I go to Hobby Lobby. ;)

We have lived in plenty, and we have lived in want. Sometimes we've been a little in over our heads—mostly my fault. But God has always provided. About five years into our marriage, I finally got pregnant, and we'd always desired that I'd stay home.

I don't want to get into the mommy wars. Again, that's something you figure out as a couple. We haven't lived close to family in a long time, so we didn't have the backup for help if I went back to work. But kudos to you if you have that support system and can make that work. We felt God calling me to be a stay-at-home mom.

But again, I liked money. I usually had two jobs, so it was very hard for me to quit. I worked until the day I had Braydee. I still don't know how we made it, but God multiplied the little we had and somehow, we never went without a thing. Someone was always taking us to eat or bringing goodies from their garden. We even had a couple who took us to Disney World with them every year!! God called me to be a stay-at-home parent, and He provided everything we needed. It has been a wonderful experience, and I wouldn't change a thing. And He'll do it for you, too!

So, take it from me (and the Bible), trust God with your finances. He will provide. Money is no issue for Him. He wants our hearts and our obedience.

And in honor of Mark and Peggy Hayman, I can honestly say, in 20 years of marriage, Sam has never even remotely raised his voice at me! And believe me, I've given him plenty of reason to!

xoxo

Zach and Sarah Lloyd

Zach and Sarah Lloyd are husband and wife. Zach serves as pastor of East La Follette Baptist Church in La Follette, TN. He spent 175 days in Vanderbilt University Medical Center while battling COVID-19 and undergoing a double lung transplant. While all this was happening in East La Follette and Nashville TN, God was moving in a mighty way in Chattanooga, TN.

I want us to bless a Tennessee pastor in a similar way that the North American Mission Board (NAMB) blesses a church/pastor at the NAMB luncheon that we attend every summer during the Southern Baptist Convention.

In 2020, our Red Bank Baptist Church family gave three times more to our benevolent offering than they had in previous years. It was the largest benevolent offering we had ever received. We were able to help hundreds of families in our community. As our leadership was trying to navigate our church through the choppy waters of COVID-19, I wanted to lead us to do something that would show our love for one another. I grew tired of being involved in the same conversations, such as:

> Pastor, if you require masks, then my family is not coming back to church. Pastor, if you don't require masks, then my family is not coming back to church.

I was so over it. So, I sat our lead team down and said,

> "I want us to bless a Tennessee pastor in a similar way that the North American Mission Board (NAMB) blesses a church

and/or pastor at the NAMB luncheon that we attend every summer during the Southern Baptist Convention."

We made a call to our state executive director, Dr. Randy Davis, and asked if he knew of any pastor who was affected by COVID-19 that we could help. Dr. Davis connected us with Zach and Sarah Lloyd.

We wanted to bless the Lloyds with a financial gift that would be helpful. After contacting Zach's dad, we learned that one way we could bless them was to pay on their mortgage. The dollar amount we had available was enough to pay for nine months of the Lloyds' mortgage. What a blessing it was informing Sarah Lloyd that God provided money to pay nine months of their mortgage. How true is the simple child's prayer, "God is great! God is good!" Needless to say, Sarah's tears of thanksgiving and joy brought us all to tears as well.

Here is the part where "you can't outgive God" comes into play; that is, God is more generous than we will ever be. I was adamant about our leadership keeping quiet what God was able to do through us for the Lloyds. We are not in the business of spreading everyone's business. God had other plans.

It never crossed my mind that in the year 2021 the Southern Baptist Convention annual meeting would be held in Nashville, TN. It never crossed my mind that more messengers would register and attend the 2021 SBC annual meeting than had in the last twenty-five years. It never crossed my mind that I would be asked to be nominated as the Treasurer (yeah, the person who is in charge of the finances) of the 2022 SBC Pastors Conference to be voted on at the SBC annual meeting in Nashville. It never crossed my mind that NAMB President, Kevin Ezell, would call Dr. Randy Davis and ask if there were any pastors in Tennessee that they could bless at the NAMB luncheon during the convention in that same Nashville. It never crossed my mind that Dr. Davis would tell Kevin Ezell Zach's story and how Red Bank Baptist Church paid nine months of their mortgage. It never crossed my mind that Kevin would reach out to me and ask if I would participate with NAMB in telling the story of the Lloyds via video at the luncheon. It never crossed my mind that Kevin would ask me to join Dr. Davis and Zach on the platform at the luncheon to be interviewed by Kevin. It never crossed my mind that the very thing I said to our lead team eight months earlier about wanting to bless a Tennessee pastor, similar to how NAMB does at the luncheon, would result in me literally being a part of it. It never crossed my mind that the actual vote for the Treasurer of the 2022 SBC Pastors Conference, which I was one of two nominees, would happen immediately after the NAMB luncheon where I was on the platform. It never crossed my mind what a small act of generosity would do and is still doing.

To be generous is to be like Jesus. To be generous in and through marriage is to be like Jesus and His church. Generosity helps to generate a right view of theology, missiology, soteriology, ecclesiology, and eschatology. Be a generous husband. Be a generous wife. Be a generous couple. Generosity is contagious. Pass it on!

GOSPEL CONVERSATIONAL MARRIAGE

Category	Budget Amount	Amount Spent	Difference	Notes
Mortgage/Rent				
Health Insurance				
Car Loan				
Groceries				
Electricity				
Gas				
Phone				
Other				
Etc.				

SAM & TONYA GREER

CONVERSATION STARTERS

1. What has to happen for you to leave the tent of discontentment and live in the tent of contentment?

2. How do you and your spouse currently view money? Is it yours? Is it hers? Is it his? How should you view money?

3. Together, build a basic budget. See the simple budget sample at the end of this chapter. Talk about your money. Discuss with your spouse financial dreams and goals.

4. Decide to be generous to your spouse. Make a list of ways that you can be generous together.

Conversation 6

Marriages that Can

Do nothing from selfish ambition or conceit, but in humility count others more significant than yourselves. Let each of you look not only to his own interests but also to the interests of others.
Philippians 2:3-9

What is the key to having a marriage that can? Are people in good marriages just lucky? How can we improve communication in marriage? How can we resolve conflict in marriage?

Your Marriage "Can" Even When You "Can't"

It was one of those "I can't even. [insert GIF of your choice] I just can't" type of moments. The second day of the 2019 Southern Baptist Convention in Birmingham, Alabama was shaping up to be a fantastic day. Our Red Bank Baptist Church staff and spouses, who were in attendance, had breakfast together and headed over to the business session for a very important vote, perhaps the most important vote in recent years; that is, a vote to approve the Committee on Nominations Report. How exciting, right? Sure, the SBC messengers vote on this report every year at the convention. So, what was so special about this report? In short, my name was included in the report!

The Committee on Nominations Report includes all the trustee nominations for all SBC entities. The International Mission Board of Trustees was included, and I was one of the pastors nominated to be a trustee. Serving on the IMB Trustee Board was my first opportunity to serve as a part of an SBC entity, and I was pumped.

The SBC way of voting can be summed up by the words "raise your ballots." More specifically,

"All in favor of the Committee on Nominations Report, raise your ballots. Thank you. Any in opposition, raise your ballots. Thank you."

The voting process seemed simple enough, or so I thought. On our way over to the business session I asked all of our staff and spouses:

"Do you have your ballots?"

Everyone affirmed they had their ballot in their hand except for one, my wife Tonya.

Tonya responded:

"I put my ballot in my purse and I can't get it out because I just painted my nails and they are still wet. Can you get it for me?"

If it were possible for Tonya to lose her salvation, she would lose it in her purse.

Soon after we took our seats in the general session, President J.D. Greear called for the vote to affirm the report by saying:

"All in favor of affirming the report raise your ballots."

We all raised our ballots. Well, almost all of us raised our ballots. Tonya was fumbling around with her ballot, because, of all things, her nails were still wet, and she missed the opportunity to vote for the report.

Then it happened. After calling for votes in favor of the report, President Greear said:

"Any in opposition to the report, raise your ballots."

In a room of thousands of people, one ballot shot up in the air at that very moment, Tonya's ballot. After fumbling with her ballot, Tonya was somehow able, even with wet nails, to gain her composure and lift her ballot up in the air at the exact moment those in opposition were asked to raise their ballots. By voting against the motion, Tonya voted against me! That's right, she not only didn't vote *for* me, she voted *against* me! I love my wife. She is my crown.

Even *marriages that can* experience "I just can't" moments. Even amidst those "I just can't" moments, you can still have a *marriage that can*. In fact, all marriages have "I can't even" moments. All marriages have conflict. All marriages need communication improvement. All marriages are a work in progress. How can you have a *marriage that can*?

Keys That Unlock a Marriage That Can

Y'all, we have it backwards. We cry tears of sadness at Christian funerals and rejoice with gladness at Christian weddings. This should not be! A reversal is in order. We should be rejoicing with gladness at that funeral of any and every person saved by grace. Whosoever dies in Christ doesn't go to a "better place," but the "best place."

Visualize the following hypothetical situation taking place after the death of the repentant thief on the cross. What if the repentant thief, who died next to Jesus on the cross the same day Jesus died, had a funeral? What would the officiating pastor say at said funeral? Perhaps, the pastor might say:

Dearly beloved, we are gathered here today to bury
this unknown guy who never darkened the door of a church (synagogue), never went to Sunday School, never went to Vacation Bible School, never read the Torah (the Bible), never was baptized, never partook of the Lord's Supper, never pressed his luck by eating food at a church potluck, never went to a fifth Sunday singing, never served as a deacon, never went on Tuesday night visitation, never prayed at Wednesday night prayer meeting, never tithed, never went on an international mission trip, never went on a national mission trip, never went on any mission trip, never gave to Lottie Moon or Annie Armstrong, never served on the Disaster Relief Team, never led a small group, never was discipled by anyone, never discipled anyone, yet, HE MADE IT INTO PARADISE WITH JESUS! HE MADE IT INTO HEAVEN!

Meanwhile in heaven, an angel asks this unknown thief:

"Why are you here? How did you get here?"

The thief replies:

"I don't know."

The angel forcefully asks:

"What do you mean you don't know?"

The thief reiterates:

"Because, I don't know!"

Finally, the angel asks:

"On what basis are you here?"

The thief explains:

"The man on the middle cross said I can come."[xxx]

Don't you imagine that there would be much shouting for joy and rejoicing at a funeral like that? Absolutely! We should rejoice with gladness at Christian funerals and shed tears of sadness at Christian weddings.

I am batting 1000 officiating funerals that last and less than .500 presiding over weddings that last.

Wait, shed tears of sadness at weddings? Who has ever heard of such nonsense? Let me explain before you cancel me. We should cry tears of sadness at weddings because the man and the woman standing at the altar reciting their vows have no idea what's coming. Sadly, many of the weddings I have officiated have been undone via divorce. Never once has any funeral I officiated been undone. I am batting 1000 officiating funerals that last and less than .500 presiding over weddings that last.

Tonya and I are both tired of seeing *marriages that can't* and want to see more *marriages that can*. What makes for a lasting marriage? What makes marriage last? Are there any keys to unlocking *marriages that can*?

We posed the following question to our Red Bank Baptist and The Point church family:

What is the key(s) to unlocking a marriage that can?

Here are some responses you may find helpful:

- Commit to Jesus, His Word, and each other.

- Be a gentleman. Open doors.

- Love each other even when you don't like each other.

- Don't withhold affection as a weapon.

- Patience, patience, patience.

- Talk and walk. Walk and talk.

- Never give up.

- Be kind to one another. Respect one another.

- Learn the difference between listening and fixing.

- Seek to be righteous rather than right.

- What money we have is "ours" not "mine."

- Pray together.

- Arguing may lead to fights. Fights must lead to reconciliation.

GOSPEL CONVERSATIONAL MARRIAGE

- Both parties must understand that she wants security while he wants respect and sex.

- God first, then marriage squished right up there next to Him.

- Honest communication.

- Cheer each other on.

- Put yourself last and spouse first.

- Children third, spouse second, and God first.

- Think before you speak.

- Be willing to give and take.

- Be each other's Aaron when the other is Moses.

- Husband, step up and lead. Wife, submit and follow.

- Say "I love you," "I am sorry," and "forgive me."

- You can't put your spouse first one time. You can't say "I love you" one time. You can't pray for your spouse one time. You can't fill their tank one time, but you must do all these things every single day.

Which one of these keys do you need to work on in your marriage? Stop reading and write down three of these keys that need some work on your part. What other keys to unlocking a *marriage that can* would you add to the list above? Stop reading and make a list of other keys you would add.

Philippians 2:4 is the key to unlocking a *marriage that can*.

One key sums up most, if not all, of the keys listed above. It is a biblical principle we find in both the Old and New Testament. Love God. Love people. Jesus identified these as the first and second greatest commandments. In Philippians 2:4, Paul shows what this looks like in a believer's life:

Let each of you look not only to his own interests, but also to the interests of others.

How does this shake out in marriage? A husband, who puts the interests of his wife before his own, and a wife, who puts the interests of her husband before her own, will experience marriage the way God intended. Why? Because they are not looking out for self; rather, they are looking out for spouse. I know Philippians 2:4 was not written in the context of marriage. What better opportunity, however, to display this biblical principle than in the context of marriage? Philippians 2:4 is the key to unlocking a *marriage that can*.

Wedding at Cana Holds the Key to Marriages That Can

What is the worst thing that can happen before, during, or after a wedding? A groom in Southwest Florida was arrested in July 2021 for attacking wedding guests on his wedding day at his own wedding. Lee county deputies arrived on the scene to find Jeffery Johnson being restrained by wedding guests. Johnson turned his aggression toward the deputies and was taken to jail. He was charged with two counts of battery on law enforcement officers. Johnson spent his wedding night in jail. Under the category of worst things that can happen after a wedding, a groom being arrested ranks fairly high.[xxxi]

What is the worst thing that can happen during a wedding? I was officiating a wedding of a twin whose brother was the best man. During the wedding ceremony, I kept calling the groom by his twin brother's name. Totally embarrassing. One of the worst things that could ever happen at a 1st century Jewish wedding happened at the wedding at Cana attended by Jesus, His mother, and His disciples. John 2:1-11 records the account:

On the third day there was a wedding at Cana in Galilee, and the mother of Jesus was there. Jesus also was invited to the wedding with his disciples. When the wine ran out, the mother of Jesus said to him, "They have no wine." And Jesus said to her, "Woman, what does this have to do with me? My hour has not yet come." His mother said to the servants, "Do whatever he tells you." Now there were six stone water jars there for the Jewish rites of purification, each holding twenty or thirty gallons. Jesus said to his servants, "Fill the jars with water." And they filled them up to the brim. And he said to them, "Now draw some out and take it to the master of the feast." So they took it. When the master of the feast tasted the water now become wine, and did not know where it came from (though the servants who had drawn the water knew), the master of the feast called the bridegroom and said to him, "Everyone serves the good wine first, and when people have drunk freely, then the poor wine. But you have kept the good wine until now." This, the first of his signs, Jesus did at Cana in Galilee, and manifested his glory. And his disciples believed in him.

Running out of wine at a 1st century Jewish wedding, which was exactly what occurred at the wedding at Cana, was one of the worst things that could happen. What a social disaster that would've stained this couple and their families for the rest of their lives. The groom and his family would be held responsible, and a lawsuit from the bride's family would be a reasonable possibility. Imagine having a wedding full of guests but with no food, no cake, no beverages, no celebration, no music, no reception, and no joy. How would you like to be known through history as the only couple in your city whose wedding was joyless? Stop the madness!

First century Jewish marriage feasts were intended to be joyous occasions. Running out of wine at a 1st century Jewish wedding was the same as running out of joy. From a Hebraic worldview, wine was the personification of joy. The Old Testament Scriptures support the realization of wine symbolizing joy. In Judges 9:13, the Bible says:

But the vine said to them, "Shall I leave my wine that cheers God and men and go hold sway over the trees?"

The Psalmist wrote in Psalm 104:15:

...and wine to gladden the heart of man, oil to make his face shine and bread to strengthen man's heart.

Isaiah the prophet wrote in Isaiah 55:1:

Come, everyone who thirsts, come to the waters; and he who has no money; come, buy and eat! Come, buy wine and milk without money and without price.

Isaiah 55:1 is cross referenced in Revelation 22:17 where we see a picture of the joy of Jesus' second coming, the joy of heaven, and the joy of inviting others to come to Jesus by faith. John wrote in Revelation 22:17:

The Spirit and the Bride say, "Come." And let the one who hears say, "Come." And let the one who is thirsty come; let the one who desires take the water of life without price.

GOSPEL CONVERSATIONAL MARRIAGE

We would be hard pressed to deny the joyous nature of Isaiah 55:1, which includes wine. An old Jewish saying affirms this as well:

"Without wine, there is no joy!"[xxxii]

Has your marriage run out of joy? What do you do when the joy gauge in your marriage is on empty? I stole this from somebody somewhere.

> A little boy was telling his parents about hearing the story of the wedding at Cana in Sunday School. His dad asked him:
>
> "What did you learn?"
>
> The young child thought for a moment and said:
>
> "If you are going to have a wedding, make sure Jesus is there!"

Because the couple from Cana invited Jesus to their wedding, He was able and willing to restore the joy by performing the miracle of changing water to wine. Jesus is still able. Jesus is still willing. Jesus still performs miracles. Jesus can still perform a miracle in your marriage. Just like the red wine brought joy to the wedding, Jesus' shed blood will bring joy to your marriage. You see, the same Jesus who brought joy to the wedding at Cana through the red wine is the same Jesus who will bring joy to your marriage through His red, shed blood. Invite Jesus into your life. Invite Jesus into your home. Invite Jesus into your family. Invite Jesus in into your marriage. Whatever you do and wherever you are, make sure Jesus is there!

Jesus always brings joy. Marriages are a mess. Satan messes with marriage, we make a mess of marriage, but Jesus, the Messiah, takes those messes and brings about His message. What is His message? Jesus is an equal opportunity Savior of souls. Jesus referred to His mother Mary as "woman" after she told Him they ran out of wine. Why did Jesus refer to her as "woman"? Jesus came to save men, women, boys and girls, including His own mother. Mary needed to know and understand that not only was she the mother of God the Son, but she was also a daughter of God the Father. Yes, Mary is the mother of Jesus, but Jesus is also the Savior of Mary. Just as Jesus brings joy to every soul, including Mary, He also brings joy to every marriage.

Judaism only brings judgment, but Jesus always brings joy.

At the wedding at Cana, Jesus told His servants to fill the six stone water jars, which were there for the Jewish rites of purification, with water. Then, Jesus told them to draw the water-now-become-wine out and take it to the master of the feast. The Jewish rites of purification were for ceremonial purposes only. Regarding such rites, the Pharisees even called Jesus out because His disciples weren't following their man-made rules. What a stark difference seen between Judaism and Jesus. Judaism (any form of religion) only brings judgment, while Jesus always brings joy. Marriages don't need more judgment, they need joy. All marriages experience nosedives, some marriages don't survive, but your marriage can thrive.

Do whatever he tells you. What is the best marriage advice you have ever heard? The best marriage advice I have ever heard is also the best advice I have ever heard. I heard it when I read what Mary the mother of Jesus said to the servants at the wedding at Cana in John 2:3-5:

When the wine ran out, the mother of Jesus said to him, "They have no wine." And Jesus said to her, "Woman, what does this have to do with me? My hour has not yet come." His mother said to the servants, "Do whatever he tells you."

Mary told Jesus the wine ran out. Jesus told Mary His time had not yet come. Mary told the servants to do whatever Jesus told to them to do. If a husband and wife will do what Jesus tells them to do, then they will experience a marriage that can.

The most joyous moment regarding marriage is not before marriage when a husband-to-be bows one knee before the wife-to-be, but it's during marriage when both husband and wife bow both knees to the Bridegroom.

Viewing different videos of men proposing to women is special, fun, and full of joy. Yet, the most joyous moment regarding marriage is not before marriage when a husband-to-be bows one knee before the wife-to-be, but it's during marriage when both husband and wife bow both knees to the Bridegroom. It happens as both husband and wife decide to do what Jesus says. Examine any marriage. Dissect it. Break it down and the breakdown happens when either husband or wife are *not* doing what Jesus tells them to do. Obey God's Word! Period! Facts! The end! That's all folks! That's all I have to say about that!

Jesus can renew your marriage right now. In the New Testament, Jesus' first reference to "His hour" was to His mother at the wedding, and His last reference to "His hour" was to his Father in the Garden of Gethsemane. Why did Jesus tell his mother that "His hour" had not yet come? Jesus submitted to His Father's will not His mother's will. So, why did Jesus move ahead with the miracle of changing water to wine? Jesus performed this miracle for at least three reasons: (1) He restored a messy wedding on the verge of a social catastrophe, (2) He revealed the glory of His Father, and (3) He believed His disciples would believe in Him. Watch this! All three of those reasons were for someone other than Jesus: (1) the bride and groom, (2) His Father, and (3) His disciples. Jesus always performed miracles for the benefit of others, not to amaze the crowds with His power.

First, Jesus knew the bride and groom's wedding needed to be restored. Guess what? Jesus knows that your marriage needs to be renewed right now. Jesus cares about your marriage and He wants it to be renewed. Our Lord Jesus is in the restoration business not the demolition business. Jesus can and will renew your marriage right now just like He renewed the wedding at Cana. You must want Him to renew it. You must believe He will. You must trust Him to do so. Stop and pray. Ask God to renew your marriage. If your spouse is not a believer, then ask Jesus to make him or her new right now. Ask the Holy Spirit to renew your marriage right now.

Second, Jesus knew by performing this miracle that His Father would get all the glory.

BREAKING NEWS:

Your marriage is bigger than you, it's not about you, and it's not for you!

When your marriage is renewed by Jesus, the Holy Spirit will then use your testimony to glorify His Father. In order for the Holy Spirit to use your testimony, you must share your testimony. God wants you to share your marriage renewal miracle with other married couples. How are you and your spouse leveraging your marriage to promote God's glory? What do you need to do differently to highlight the glory of God in and through your marriage?

It's not that Jesus believes in you. It's that Jesus believes that you will believe in Him.

Lastly, Jesus also knew that His disciples would believe in Him. The world is lying to you. Satan is lying to you. Your flesh is lying to you. The world, Satan and your flesh all tell you to believe in yourself. Some have wrongly said, "Jesus believes in you." Believe me, Jesus doesn't believe in you. In John 17:20 Jesus prayed to His Father:

I do not ask for these only, but also for those who will believe in me through their word.

It's not that Jesus believes in you. It's that Jesus believes that you will believe in Him. What a gospel! What a Savior! Jesus believes that your marriage can be renewed by Him. Do you believe that? Do you believe Jesus?

1 Corinthians 13 Is for Marriages That Can

Whew! It's a good thing that 1 Corinthians 13 is only for weddings because it's been a minute since most of us have read the "love chapter," and it shows. Sorry, I am being sarcastic. Have you noticed that 1 Corinthians 13 is for weddings what Psalm 23 is for funerals? The truth is that 1 Corinthians 13 is more for marriages than weddings. Yet, we hear it more at weddings than we see it in marriages. Paul wrote in 1 Corinthians 13:4-8, 13:

Love is patient and kind; love does not envy or boast; it is not arrogant or rude. It does not insist on its own way; it is not irritable or resentful; it does not rejoice at wrongdoing, but rejoices with the truth. Love bears all things, believes all things, hopes all things, endures all things. Love never ends...So now faith, hope, and love abide, these three; but the greatest of these is love.

Love never ends because God is love, and He never ends.

Sometimes being in a marriage can be lonelier than the third verse of a hymn. Shout out to my friend Dr. Matt Henslee for the "lonelier than the third verse of a hymn" part. Marriage shouldn't be lonely. It should be loving. Love bears, believes, hopes, and endures. Hence, love is alive and active. Love is more realized not in the BIG moments but the everyday moments, like striving to communicate better and resolving conflict. How can you and your spouse communicate better? How can you and your spouse resolve conflict? Where do you start?

Communication Is Key to a Marriage That Can

Ladies and gentlemen, we are different. Men and women communicate differently. Men communicate to maintain independence, while women communicate to maintain intimacy. Generally, men say as little as possible, while women say as much as...you crazy! I ain't going there! Men communicate to report facts and figures, while women communicate for rapport in relationships. Men tend to talk more in public, while women tend to talk more in private. Men make less eye contact, while women make more eye contact. Men don't stand too close to men, while women stand close to one another. Men communicate to fix a problem, while women communicate to understand. It's so important to understand that husband and wife don't communicate in the same way. Learn one another's love languages, and start speaking one another's language.

Speak Your Spouse's Language

One of my most rewarding preaching experiences was also one of the most intimidating. I was invited to preach a peace rally in Bangante, Cameroon. The one crowd that gathered consisted of people from three different languages: (1) French, (2) English, and (3) a certain African dialect. I don't speak French. I don't speak any African dialect. I barely speak English. I speak *redneck* English. What do you do when you only speak 1/3 of the languages represented at such a peace rally? You utilize interpreters who speak the other two languages. That's right, I preached using not one but two interpreters. It took not double the amount of time to preach a message but triple the amount of time. I was so grateful that the Holy Spirit just took over and many were saved. Why were they saved? Because they were able to hear the gospel in their own language. What if I had preached with no interpreters? Communication would've broken down and only English-speaking Africans would have heard the gospel.

Speaking any people's language is more than dialect, it is also about what makes them tick. What are they passionate about? What do they love? What is their love language? I will never forget his words. Pastor George Tanya Mbongko of Pillar and Buttress Ministry in Cameroon, Africa said,

"One Bangante Cameroonian coming to Christ is equivalent to one-hundred Muslims coming to Christ."[xv]

Why would Pastor George make such a statement? You see, the Bangante people are deceived by the darkness of ancestral worship known as the worship of the skulls.

Skull worship consists of family members burying their dead only to dig them up a year later. Upon exhuming the dead, the family removes the skulls and places them in clay pots or house-like tombs in their homes. Removing the skulls of ancestors, placing them in the home, and feeding them is based upon the belief that appeasing the ancestors of the skulls will keep evil away. The Bangante believe that improper care of ancestral skulls leads to ancestral wrath, family illness, infertility, or even death.[xvi]

In preparation to preach at the January 2016 Peace Rally in Bangante Cameroon, I listened to the pastors in Bangante share about the darkness of skull worship. Prior to the first night of the rally, I was overcome as the pastors shared that nearly every home in Bangante was full of skulls. While sitting on the preaching platform worshiping with those pastors, God moved my heart to the rich man and Lazarus text in Luke 16:19-31. God gave me a specific word to preach to the hundreds of Bangante people gathered that night. God empowered me to speak their language, not their dialect, but their love language.

When the rich man and Lazarus died, immediately, they were both alive. One was alive in Hades. One was alive at Abraham's side. In Luke 16:22-25, the Bible says:

*The poor man died and was carried by the angels to Abraham's side. The rich man also died and was buried, and in Hades, being in torment, he lifted up his eyes and saw Abraham far off and Lazarus at his side. And he called out, '****Father*** *Abraham, have mercy on me, and send Lazarus to dip the end of his finger in water and cool my tongue, for I am in anguish in this flame.' But Abraham said, '****Child****, remember that you in your lifetime received your good things, and Lazarus in like manner bad things; but now he is comforted here, and you are in anguish. And besides all this, between us and you a great chasm has been fixed, in order that those who would pass from here to you may not be able, and none may cross from there to us.'*

The rich man's use of "father" and Abraham's use of "child" offered a Holy Spirit-inspired opportunity for practical gospel application. Often, I have pondered the use of these two familial terms in the context of Luke 16. As I was sitting on the Peace Rally platform, while praying over the Bangante people enslaved by ancestral worship, God gave me this clear insight. The reason the rich man referred to Abraham as "father" was because Abraham was his Jewish ancestor. The reason Abraham referred to the rich man as "child" was because the rich man was his Jewish descendant. To hear the ancestor of ancestors, Abraham, tell his descendant "between us and you a great chasm has been fixed" is a terrifying truth. Basically, the rich man was being told that his ancestor could do nothing for him.

Standing before the Bangante people I said:

If the ancestor of ancestors, Abraham, was unable to do anything for his descendant, then your ancestors are unable to do anything for you. But there is One who said, "Before Abraham was I AM." Jesus wants you to know that before the ancestor of ancestors was, He said, "I AM." Jesus wants you to know that He put skull worship to death through His death at the place called the Skull. Jesus invites you to forsake skull worship and trust in Him alone as your Savior and follow Him as Lord.

Some accepted the invitation, and some did not. But all understood because I was intentional about speaking their language.

What happens when you don't speak your spouse's language? Communication breaks down and you and your spouse lose the connection like a dropped Zoom call. Do you know your love language? Do you know your spouse's love language? Read Gary Chapman's book, *The Five Love Languages*, and start speaking your spouse's language. Jesus spoke the language of the people with whom He spoke. Jesus spoke to the Samaritan woman at the well about water, not fishing. Jesus spoke to the fishermen about fishing, not plumbing. Jesus spoke to the hungry crowds about bread, not about the Law. Jesus spoke to the teachers of the Law about the Law, not about water, fishing, or bread. Why did Jesus share the gospel in all these different ways? Jesus spoke the language of the people with whom He spoke because He loved them. Learn the love language of your spouse and speak it loud and clear!

Communication in Your Marriage

Five levels of communication are important to identify and recognize: (1) Clichés or Pleasantries, (2) Facts or Reporting, (3) Opinions or What I Think, (4) Feelings or What I Feel, and (5) Needs or

Speak the Truth in Love. You and your spouse need to ask the question:

"What is the level of our communication?"

Level one is communication at the shallowest level.

"How was your day?" "Fine."

Level two is a simple stating of the facts.

"I will be late for dinner."

Level three is an expression of what you think.

"I think we should save more money."

Level four is an expression of how you feel.

"I feel like we need to spend more time together."

Level five allows you to be honest and open.

"I haven't been leading well lately and I want to do better."

All five of these levels of communication are important and a certain amount of time should be spent on each one. How much time do you and your spouse spend on each one? Write down on the blanks provided what percentage of 100 you think y'all spend at each level. You may spend 20% on all five, or you may spend more or less on one than the others. Do this exercise individually. Don't cheat! Compare and then discuss with one another.

GOSPEL CONVERSATIONAL MARRIAGE

What's Our Level?[xxxiii]

1) CLICHÉS   _____ % of the time

2) FACTS   _____ % of the time

3) OPINIONS _____ % of the time

4) FEELINGS _____ % of the time

5) NEEDS   _____ % of the time

    Tell him. Tell her. Tell him how you feel. Tell her what you think. Tell her how you feel about her. Tell him how you like when he does this or that. Tonya didn't know about one of my favorite marriage moments from conversation four in this book. Why? I had never told her.

    Every marriage can improve in the realm of communication. So, what is keeping you from improving? What is your problem, on your part not your spouse's part, when it comes to communication in your marriage? Check any of the following statements that express problems *on your part* in your communication. Husband, check any boxes under "Him." Wives, check any boxes under "Her." Discuss your answers with one another.

What's My Problem?[xxxiv]

Him   Her

☐   ☐   I can't seem to find the right words.

☐   ☐   I'm afraid of being rejected.

☐	☐	I'm not convinced it will help if I talk.
☐	☐	I'm afraid my opinion is wrong.
☐	☐	I'm sometimes too angry to talk.
☐	☐	Speaking up only makes things worse.
☐	☐	I talk too much.
☐	☐	I lack good communication with God.
☐	☐	I try to hide the truth.
☐	☐	My speech is often defensive.
☐	☐	I frequently bring up my spouse's past.
☐	☐	My actions don't match what I say.
☐	☐	I don't really listen well.
☐	☐	I try to repay anger with anger.
☐	☐	I tease my mate too much.

Fantastic! You're already improving your communication.

Tonya and I attended as many marriage retreats as possible when we were first married. On one such retreat, we were blessed by the marriage ministry of Mark and Peggy Hayman. The Haymans shared the following ten ways to improve communication that Tonya still follows. Oops, I mean Tonya and I still follow. Sorry, Boo Boo.

Ways to Improve Communication in Your Marriage[xxxv]

1. Don't assume you know, ask.
2. Provide an open, permissive and accepting atmosphere.
3. Use compliments freely.
4. Pray for each other and together.
5. Be willing to disagree but in a gentle way.
6. Concentrate on being a good listener.
7. Build up your mate's self-esteem.
8. Seek more to understand than to be understood.
9. Ask for forgiveness.
10. Say "I love you" and "I'm sorry."

If we are going to see more *marriages that can*, then husbands and wives must listen quickly, speak wisely, diffuse anger, reconcile immediately, and speak lovingly.

Conflict in Your Marriage

Good marriages don't have problems. Myth. Conflict hurts a marriage. Myth. Husband and wives in good marriages are just lucky. Myth. All marriages have problems. Fact. Conflict can hurt a marriage but doesn't have to. Fact. Husbands and wives in good marriages work at having good marriages. Fact.

Why does conflict occur in marriage? Sin is meistic. Sin makes it all about me. When two meistic sinners come together in marriage, they will experience conflict. Several reasons abound for why conflict occurs. Some husbands and wives are power hungry or control freaks, while some struggle with insecurity. Conflict rears its ugly head when differences in values are uncovered. Being unequally yoked has nothing to do with race but everything to do with saving grace. An unequally yoked marriage happens when a believer marries an unbeliever. Often times differences in values emerge due to being unequally yoked. Other couples are dealing with conflict from unmet needs and unrealistic expectations. Some couples are competing against one another. We are not called to compete in the race that is set before us but to complete the race. Stop competing and start completing! One of our church members said it like this:

> Marriage should not be a competition to outdo your spouse as the world teaches, it should be about out-submitting your spouse. It's not one up but one under!

What are the sources of conflict in your marriage?

Sources of Conflict in Your Marriage[xxxvi]

Rank with an N, S, or O on each item to indicate how significant these are in your marriage. Complete separately then compare and discuss your answers.

N = Never produces a conflict

S = Sometimes produces a conflict

O = Often produces a conflict

GOSPEL CONVERSATIONAL MARRIAGE

CIRCUMSTANCES:

Him　　**Her**

_____　_____ Fatigue

_____　_____ Unfulfilled Needs

_____　_____ Financial Problems

_____　_____ Busy Schedule

_____　_____ Family Background

_____　_____ Relatives

_____　_____ Lack of Fellowship w/God

_____　_____ Meals

_____　_____ Church Activities

BEHAVIOR:

Him　　**Her**

_____　_____ Unrealistic Expectations

_____　_____ Unwillingness to Communicate

_____　_____ Sarcastic Remarks

_____　_____ False Assumptions

_____　_____ Jumping to Conclusions

_____　_____ Not Being Flexible

_____	_____	Irritating Habits
_____	_____	Tactlessness (Insensitive)
_____	_____	Nagging

How you and your spouse respond to conflict is equally important as identifying its source. How do you and your spouse respond to conflict in your marriage?

Response to Conflict in Your Marriage[xxxvii]

Check any of these responses that apply to you in your marriage. Answer separately, then compare and discuss. Remember, husbands check the column under "Him," while wives check the column under "Her."

Him   **Her**

_____	_____	Yell
_____	_____	Get Angry
_____	_____	Become Aggressive
_____	_____	Compromise
_____	_____	Express Feelings
_____	_____	Withdraw
_____	_____	Get Quiet

_____   _____ Get Even

_____   _____ Try to Win

      Conflict starts in your heart. The conflict in your marriage starts in your heart. In James 4:1, James wrote:

What causes quarrels and what causes fights among you? Is it not this, that your passions are at war within you?

Praise the Lord that conflict can be resolved. You don't have to stay in a state of conflict. Jesus wants you to resolve conflict and 1 Corinthians 13 is a great place to start. You may have heard 1 Corinthians 13 at your wedding, but have you seen it in your marriage? 1 Corinthians 13 wasn't written to give us warm and fuzzy feelings during a wedding ceremony. It was written to give us action steps on the battlefield of marriage. Here are a few ways to apply 1 Corinthians 13 in your marriage.

Ways to Resolve Conflict in Your Marriage[xxxviii]

1. Start with you and God.//
2. Don't let problems fester.
3. Don't air your dirty laundry on social media.
4. Don't keep bringing it up.
5. Attack the problem, not the person.
6. Don't wait for your mate to apologize first.

7. Don't overreact.

8. Clearly define the issue at hand.

9. Make sure you resolve the issue.

List at least three of these ways above that you promise to spend more time doing. List them separately, then share with your spouse and discuss.

She Says

When I was growing up, my dad would always argue with me. No matter what I said, it was always wrong. Whatever I was venting about at the moment, he would find some other way to look at my problem by asking me questions. As much as I hate to admit it, it made me think. But it was sneaky and irritated me to no end.

Now I do that to my girls. Yes, I have become my dad. Ouch! I catch myself doing it all the time and yes, they get just as irritated as I did. Yesterday I was driving Braydee to her kickboxing class and she was telling me all about something that had happened on her first day of high school. I don't even remember what it was, but to be honest, I was down-right proud of how she handled this particular situation. But I didn't tell her that. Instead I asked her questions and made it look like she could have handled it differently. As I'm doing it, I'm cursing myself for irritating my kid like my dad always did to me.

But my kid is so much cooler than me. She stops talking for a minute and looks at me with this big grin on her face and says, "Momma, every time you disagree with me, I know you are right. And I'm trying to figure out how I got it all wrong." Whoa. I did not expect that. Matter of fact, I totally agreed with her, but I guess I just want her to be able to look at everything from another perspective. Not just her own.

Our own experiences mold who we are and how we think. It's so important to understand this in marriage. Because looking at things from another perspective can help you relate better to other people. I play the same devil's advocate with Sam, too. Gosh, I just can't help myself. I've become my dad! Proverbs 21:9 tells us,

Better to live on the corner of a roof than to share a house with a nagging wife.

Ouch! Are you a nagging wife? Are you always finding ways to irritate your family? Would your family rather sit in the scorching heat and weather the wind and rain than be in the house with you?

Dr. Phil often asks couples how much fun they are to live with. I think that's the simplest question I've ever heard, but it's absolutely brilliant! So ask yourself, how much fun am I? Do I make everyone miserable? If the answer is yes, what can you do to change that? Because you CAN change it. Right now, today.

Us Greers have a lot of fun at our house. Sam and I LOVE to embarrass our teenaged daughters. It's so easy, I mean EVERY-THING is embarrassing when you are 12 and 14. And we've learned the absolute most mortifying thing to a teenage girl—they HATE when we flirt in front of them. Yes, I still flirt with my man after 20 years of marriage!

Am I a little too Type A about the cleanliness of our house and a little too hard on the girls for not meeting my demands? Sure. Sometimes. We all have our vices. I could tell you everyone's vices in our house. Even our moody cat, Oliver's and our insecure dog, Bailey's. Bailey is the most perfect dog in all of creation, but that poor soul lives in sheer terror that we are gonna leave her and never come back. She won't even go to the bathroom by herself. Drives me absolutely nuts on those frigid winter mornings.

I bet everyone in your family falls short somewhere too. It's easy to focus on what we don't like about our spouses and kids, but we should be intentional in figuring what you DO like about your family.

It's hard finding stuff everyone in a house can all enjoy. At our house we all like a couple of things—playing Spades and watching movies. To make fun of Braydee we call Spades "Spears" at our house. For some reason Braydee could never remember the word Spades so she always called it "Spears." Does your family have inside jokes? Do you have fun? Have fun in your house! Will your family ever stop being so annoying so you can have fun? No. No they won't. But you can overlook those things that don't matter and still have fun. You can look for the good and try to overlook some of the not so good.

Sam is a genius at looking for the good in all things. I wish I could be more like him. He's such a great leader in our family. Sometimes I'll come to bed ranting about something silly the girls did to drive me nuts (have I mentioned I can be a little dramatic sometimes?). Sam will listen for a while, and then he'll find some way to make fun of it. The next thing I know, I'm laughing too.

Every morning when I wake up, I open the blinds. Every evening when Sam gets home, he closes the blinds. Every evening I turn on the lamps. Every morning, Sam turns off the lamps. I turn the air up, Sam turns the air down. Every morning Braydee spills her oatmeal on the floor, every morning I sweep up the oatmeal. I swear that kid spills more oatmeal than she eats. Belle leaves her peppermint candy wrappers (from Ms. Barbara's desk at church) all over the floor, I pick up said wrappers. Every. Single. Day. That kid can put down some peppermint from Ms. Barbara's office!

Point is, there are things that will annoy you about your spouse and kids. But ask yourself, "Is this worth ruining the joy of the day? Is this a battle worth fighting?" If not, let it go. Pick up that candy wrapper for the seven-millionth time, and bite your tongue. It will be ok!

Every time Sam and I go on a trip, I always forget socks. He has learned over the years to always bring an extra pair of socks so I won't freeze slam to death or dirty up all of his. Every Saturday I refill Sam's supplement box with his daily vitamins. Braydee unloads the dishwasher, and Belle feeds our livestock. What can you do to serve your spouse and family and make your family work better? Give those kids chores! Let them help. Will they complain sometimes? Absolutely. But let them have ownership of being part of the family unit. Too often in our households, the parents serve the kids. Let them serve YOU! Teaching Braydee to vacuum and Belle to dust this past summer has been life changing! If you want to pay them an allowance to help them learn how money works, great. But it's not necessary. Everyone needs to pitch in to make the house run so not just one person carries too much of the load. Philippians 2:4 tells us,

Let each of you look not only to his own interests, but also to the interests of others.

    I love this scripture, it doesn't tell us to neglect ourselves and only look out for others, but it tells us to look after others, too. In your marriage, look out for each other. If something isn't really your thing but your spouse or kids get excited about it, get excited with them and try it out. Who knows, maybe you'll have something else you enjoy doing together.

Here's our family chore list. I started it this summer, and we keep it on the fridge:

Summer Rules

1. To bed by midnight
2. Up by 9 a.m.
3. No eating after 8 p.m.
4. Have a fruit and veggie daily
5. Clean up after yourself and your guests
6. Screen time rules stand. No asking for more time
7. Read daily
8. Read a chapter from the book of John every day

9. One hour of exercise M-F
10. No screen time until chores and exercise done
11. Everyone gets chores this summer, not just momma

Chores

Belle:

Braydee:

Clean, test & treat the pool
Your laundry
Make your bed when you get up
Water plants/shrubs
Pick up after yourself
Feed the pets
Straighten the couch at night
Dust

Vacuum carpet
Clean your bathroom
Do your own laundry
Empty the dishwasher
Wipe kitchen appliances
Make your bed when you get up
Straighten the couch and living room

And for the love of all things holy, please don't let me step on crumbs when I get up in the morning.

We will enter Middle/High school healthy: mentally, physically and spiritually. Boundaries are healthy for us. Guard your hearts and minds. Pay attention to who your friends are.

xoxo

My Arms Don't Work

    I try to be a patient guy. I make an intentional attempt to be understanding and kind. Until, well, something like what happened on a recent Ocoee whitewater rafting trip goes down. Whitewater rafting is the most fun activity one can engage in on planet earth. Rafting through whitewater is where "work hard" and "play hard" collide. The work is work. Rafting guides aren't shy about shouting different commands: "Forward two! Back two! Get down!" When you hear those commands, your paddle is in motion.

Yes, both work and play are expected and required while rafting on the Ocoee. Or, are they? On this particular rafting trip, Tonya and I were added to a raft of four people. We had six not counting the guide. As all the rafters boarded a bus to be taken to the river, I noticed that two of the ladies who were on our raft didn't have paddles. I thought, "That's odd." When we arrived at the river, each rafter picked up the raft together and walked toward the water. Those same two ladies who didn't have paddles didn't help us with the raft.

The youngest of the two ladies said:

"My arms don't work. That is why I don't have a paddle, and I didn't help with the raft. I am just along for the ride."

I thought to myself:

"Though they look like able bodied people, these two ladies must be disabled."

Nope, not disabled at all! On the bus, while they ate food, their arms seemed to work fine, but now that work was required their arms suddenly had amnesia.

You are not going to believe what happened next. First of all, these ladies complained the whole time that they were getting wet. About half-way through the rafting course, they told the guide they were too tired to continue. Are you kidding me? Seriously? Tired from what? They weren't paddling at all! They had no paddles to paddle! We stopped and waited for the guide to walk them up a rocky bank to the road. Our trip was delayed nearly an hour. It was an exercise in patience. I may or may not have wanted to throw them out of the boat.

What do you do when you are ready to throw your spouse out of the boat of marriage? What do you do when you are ready to throw in the towel on your marriage? What do you do when your spouse's emotional, spiritual, or relational "arms don't work"? When your husband's arms don't work, be his Aaron. When your wife's arms don't work, be her Aaron.

CONVERSATION STARTERS

1. Make a list of your own keys to unlocking a marriage that can. Compare your list with your spouse.

2. Read Philippians 2:4. In what ways are you putting your spouse before self? In what ways are you not?

3. Read John 2:1-11. Discuss how the wedding at Cana holds the key to a marriage that can.

4. Read 1 Corinthians 13. Discuss how you can improve communication and resolve conflict in your marriage with your spouse.

SAM & TONYA GREER

Conversation 7

Grace Moves Your Marriage from Good to Great

And after you have suffered a little while, the God of all grace, who has called you to his eternal glory in Christ, will himself restore, confirm, strengthen, and establish you.
1 Peter 5:10

How can your marriage on earth move from good to great? Will married couples be reunited in heaven? If marriage is the best of the best on earth, then how is heaven without marriage far better?

Best Part of the Wedding

Which part of a wedding do you like the most? Okay, second to the food, which part of the wedding is the best? Fine, second to the food and the dancing, which part of the wedding is your favorite? Yes, I am a Baptist with a capital "B," and I like to dance. I'm all about *getting jiggy with it*, *shaking what my momma gave me*, and *busting a move*.

Now I'm really showing my age...and am really good at that...and mostly good with that. Mostly.

Pastor Johnny Hunt was once asked if Baptists can dance and he replied:

"Some can and some can't."

Moving past all the "fun" stuff, what is your favorite part of a wedding ceremony? Maybe your favorite is the entrance of the bride, the reciting of vows, the exchanging of rings, the kiss, or the pronouncement of husband and wife. No doubt, the kiss is the groom's favorite part, but probably not the bride's favorite. Why does the kiss get so little press? Wedding planning, rehearsal, ceremony, reception and dress get most of the press, but what about the kiss?

Alright, let's move on, shall we? My favorite part of the wedding ceremony happens toward the beginning. After the bride and her dad (or whoever walks her down the aisle) walk down the aisle, the following question is asked by the officiate:

"Who gives [bride's name] in marriage to [groom's name]?"

The father of the bride is instructed to answer:

"Her mother and I."

Or, is it "her mother and me?"

"Her mother and I" sounds right, but grammatically is "her mother and me" right? English grammar is the worst. At least my English grammar is the worst. Anyway, after the answer is given, the groom steps down from the elevated platform and retrieves his bride.

THAT is my favorite part of any wedding! What a picture! What a picture of the gospel! What a picture of Jesus, the Bridegroom, coming back to retrieve His bride, the church! Any and every believer who witnesses a groom stepping down to retrieve his bride should rejoice in his/her heart that Jesus is coming back for His church. In the last verse of a rap song about marriage entitled "The Other Woman," I wrote:

> The Apostle Paul wrote much about dis mystery
> Christ and His church, dat is the Gospel, for all to see
> My favorite part of dat wedding ceremony
> Is when da groom comes down & gets his bride-to-be
> It's not a pic of what comes back from a google search
> But it's a picture of God coming back for His church!

Jesus is coming back! Know this beloved, His coming will be seen, soon, and it is sure. Come, Lord Jesus!

How can we know for sure that Jesus is coming? First of all, Jesus told us that He *is* the truth, which means we *can* trust Him. Also, we can know Jesus is coming back because He said so. In Revelation 22:7, Jesus said:

> *Behold, I am coming soon.*

The word *behold* in the Greek is *idou* and it means "look," "listen," "see," or "pay attention."[xxxix] Do you realize that the word *behold* is an imperative? Jesus, then, is commanding us to pay attention to the fact that He is coming soon. Are you watching and waiting for His coming? Pay attention!

Can you imagine trying to plan a wedding with no calendared date? The guest list is finalized, the wedding location is picked out, the invitations are printed, but there is no date. No date for the guests to show up, no date to secure the wedding location, and no date to put on the invitations. After the attack on Pearl Harbor, planning a wedding with no date became a reality for many American couples. In a typical scenario, a young woman became engaged to her beau who subsequently shipped out with the Navy before they could have a wedding. Until the groom-to-be had enough leave time, there would be no wedding. The bride-to-be and her mother planned the wedding down to the last detail, and they even printed invitation. But they left the date off because they didn't know when the groom would return, and they waited at the ready. Finally, after eighteen long months, a telegram, which was Instagram before Instagram, arrived that read: "You should get that white dress you've been wanting!" The groom was on his way. Jesus, our Bridegroom, is on His way; we just don't know the day.

According to Jesus, His coming will be soon. Think about that. John the revelator recorded Jesus' words over two thousand years ago. Right now, in the very moment you are reading these words, we are closer to the Second Coming of Jesus than any other time in human history. So, what should we be doing until Jesus' coming? John, the disciple whom Jesus loved, wrote in Revelation 22:17:

The Spirit and the Bride say, "Come."

The Spirit is the Holy Spirit, while the Bride is the church.

When Jesus comes, what does that mean for marriage? Will there be marriage in heaven? Will your marriage exist in heaven?

Did you catch that? The Holy Spirit and the church are both responding to the revelation that Jesus is coming with one word—"Come." Note, the world will never say to Jesus, "Come." The flesh will never say to Jesus, "Come." Satan will never say to Jesus, "Come." ONLY the Spirit and the church say, "Come, Lord Jesus!" When Jesus comes, what does that mean for marriage? Will there be marriage in heaven? Will your marriage exist in heaven?

Your Marriage Can Be Better on Earth

Before we get way ahead of ourselves thinking about marriage in heaven, let's deal with marriage on earth. God is for marriage on earth. God is for your marriage on earth. Husbands, the Bible says in Proverbs 18:22:

He who finds a wife finds a good thing and obtains favor from the Lord.

God created marriage for our good and for His glory! Marriage is a good thing. God desires for you and your spouse to have a good marriage. God loves to love. God loves to love you. God loves to love your spouse. God loves you and your spouse even when y'all don't like one another. Gospel loves to pour out His favor on you and your spouse. God favors marriage and family.

How can your marriage move from not-so-good to good, less-than-great to great, or good to great?

Do you have a good marriage? Do you have a not-so-good marriage? Do you have a great marriage? Do you have a less-than-great marriage? How can your marriage move from not-so-good to good, less-than-great to great, or good to great? Consider these five ways to move your marriage from good to great.

1. Grow in your understanding of grace.

Wherever your marriage falls on the good to great marriage scale, your marriage can be better because there's no better place to exercise grace than in marriage. For marriage is the place where God highlights His grace! In 1 Peter 3:7, the Bible says:

Likewise, husbands, live with your wives in an understanding way, showing honor to the woman as the weaker vessel, since they are heirs with you of the grace of life, so that your prayers may not be hindered.

To *live with your wives in an understanding way* and *showing honor to the woman as the weaker vessel* is grace lived out. Husbands, there's no way we can always understand our wives, but we can always live with them in an understanding way. Just as Christ cares for His church, the weaker vessel, husbands must care for their wives. Wives are not intellectually inferior to their husbands. The *weaker vessel* speaks to wives being weaker physically. Hence, the husband is to show grace and not use their strength to serve self. Wives are *heirs* with their husbands of the *grace of life,* that is, the gift of salvation.

Husbands, there's no way we can always understand our wives, but we can always live with them in an understanding way.

Wives, you are called to live in such a way that would lead unsaved husbands to the Way. Conduct yourselves as if the person closest to you, your husband, is lost and headed to hell. In 1 Peter 3:1, the Bible says;

Likewise, wives, be subject to your own husbands, so that even if some do not obey the word, they may be won without a word by the conduct of their wives.

Living in this way, from a wife's perspective, is also portraying the grace of life. Ladies, it takes much grace to submit to your husband. God alone is the only one who can give you such grace. You can't submit by grace until you first surrender to grace. Both husband and wife must grow in their understanding of grace. Marriage is the best place to grow in grace. What is grace?

Justice is "you get what you deserve." Let's say I troll you on social media and just let you have it. Then, you troll me and give it back to me. That is justice. Eye for an eye. Tweet for a tweet. Post for a post. Troll for a troll.

Mercy is "you don't get what you deserve." Same scenario but different outcome. I troll you on social media and comment negatively, but you refrain from trolling me and commenting negatively. You have exercised mercy.

Grace is "you get what you don't deserve." I troll you on social media and rip you again, but you refrain from trolling me on social media and ripping me. What's more, you buy me an iPhone 12 Pro Max (or the latest and greatest iPhone at the time you are reading this). That is grace. Grace is the undeserved, unearned, and unmerited favor of God. In such a situation, I didn't do anything deserving of you buying me a new iPhone. On the contrary, I did everything deserving of having any and every device taken away from me forever. You and I deserve Hell. We earned Hell. We merit Hell. But God gives us Heaven. God the Father gives us Jesus.

None of us have a hard time believing in a lot of grace. We believe in grace a lot. Grace is extended a lot because grace is needed a lot. The question is, do we believe in grace alone? God's grace is God's gift to the human race. God's grace reaches us. God's grace rescues us. God's grace regenerates us. God's grace readies us. God's grace repurposes us. God's grace reuses us. Paul David Tripp said:

> Grace. You need it. You can't live without it, but you can't purchase it and you can't earn it, it only ever comes by means of a gift, and when you receive it, you immediately realize how much you needed it all along, and you wonder how you could've lived so long without it. Grace reaches you where you are and takes you where God wants you to be.[xl]

God's grace remains undefeated because we are saved by grace alone, and grace alone is sufficient for believers.

In order to grow in our understanding of grace, we must understand that grace is not a New Testament idea. From the Creator God to John the Revelator, from the old heavens and old earth to the new heavens and new earth, from the sin of man to the salvation of God, from Genesis to Revelation, God's grace remains undefeated:

Genesis: The undefeated grace of God chose a sinful family line (Abraham) & promised to bless the world.

Exodus: The undefeated grace of God brought God's people out of Egypt.

Leviticus: The undefeated grace of God provided God's people with a sacrificial system to atone for their sins.

Numbers: The undefeated grace of God brought God's people to the border of the promised land not because of them but in spite of them.

Deuteronomy: The undefeated grace of God gave God's people the new land.

Joshua: The undefeated grace of God gave Israel victory after victory in their conquest of the land.

Judges: The undefeated grace of God took weak leaders and used them to purge the land of idolatry.

Ruth: The undefeated grace of God included a poverty-stricken, desolate, foreign woman in the line of Christ.

1 & 2 Samuel: The undefeated grace of God established the throne, forever, through an adulterous murderer: King David.

1 & 2 Kings: The undefeated grace of God prolonged kingly punishment for the sake of King David.

1 & 2 Chronicles: The undefeated grace of God reminded the returning exiles of God's promises to David.

Ezra: The undefeated grace of God used the powerful pagan ruler Cyrus to bring God's people back home to rebuild the temple.

Nehemiah: The undefeated grace of God provided for the rebuilding of the walls of the city.

Esther: The undefeated grace of God protected God's people from a Persian plot to eradicate them.

Job: The undefeated grace of God vindicated Job.

Psalms: The undefeated grace of God reminds us of the refuge God is for His people.

Proverbs: The undefeated grace of God opens up to us a world of wisdom leading to a life of godliness.

Ecclesiastes: The undefeated grace of God reminds us that God alone satisfies sinners.

Song of Songs: The undefeated grace of God is faintly echoed in the pleasure of faithful human intimacy.

Isaiah: The undefeated grace of God reassured God's people of His presence.

Jeremiah: The undefeated grace of God promises a new covenant.

Lamentations: The undefeated grace of God is seen in God's unfailing faithfulness.

Ezekiel: The undefeated grace of God replaced stony hearts with fleshly hearts.

Daniel: The undefeated grace of God preserved His servants in the furnace and the Lions' Den.

Hosea: The undefeated grace of God is pictured in the unstoppable love toward an unfaithful wife.

Joel: The undefeated grace of God is promised in the pouring out of God's Spirit on all flesh.

Amos: The undefeated grace of God promised restoration.

Obadiah: The undefeated grace of God promised judgment on Israel's enemy.

Jonah: The undefeated grace of God extended to both immoral Nineveh and moral Jonah, both irreligious pagans and a religious prophet, both of whom needed the grace of God.

Micah: The undefeated grace of God pardoned iniquity and passed over transgressions.

Nahum: The undefeated grace of God assured Israel of good news.

Habakkuk: The undefeated grace of God freed His people to rejoice in Him.

Zephaniah: The undefeated grace of God was demonstrated as God sang over His people.

Haggai: The undefeated grace of God is seen in God's Chosen One.

Zechariah: The undefeated grace of God pledged to open up a fountain for His people to be cleansed.

Malachi: The undefeated grace of God declared His no-strings-attached love for His people.

Matthew: The undefeated grace of God fulfilled the Old Testament promises of a coming King.

Mark: The undefeated grace of God is seen in the coming king becoming a ransom buying back sinners.

Luke: The undefeated grace of God extended to all people as the coming king came to seek and save the lost.

John: The undefeated grace of God is found by God becoming one of us and by believing in Him we have eternal life.

Acts: The undefeated grace of God is on the move from Jerusalem to the ends of the earth.

Romans: The undefeated grace of God is found in Christ alone.

1 Corinthians: The undefeated grace of God is seen in God favoring what is foolish according to the world.

2 Corinthians: The undefeated grace of God is found in God channeling His power through weaknesses rather than strengths.

Galatians: The undefeated grace of God justifies both Jew and Gentile.

Ephesians: The undefeated grace of God is seen in salvation by grace alone.

Philippians: The undefeated grace of God is realized through Christ's humiliating death on an instrument of torture.

Colossians: The undefeated grace of God is seen in the nailing to the cross the record of debt that stood against us.

1 Thessalonians: The undefeated grace of God promises that Christ will return again.

2 Thessalonians: The undefeated grace of God gives us eternal comfort.

1 Timothy: The undefeated grace of God is seen in the radical mercy shown to the chief of sinners.

2 Timothy: The undefeated grace of God begins and fuels the Christian life.

Titus: The undefeated grace of God saved us when we were most mired in sinful passions.

Philemon: The undefeated grace of God offers to us what we never deserve.

Hebrews: The undefeated grace of God presents Christ as our once for all sacrifice and our great high priest.

James: The undefeated grace of God gives us more grace.

1 Peter: The undefeated grace of God secures for us an imperishable inheritance.

2 Peter: The undefeated grace of God promises that all wrongs will be made right.

1 John: The undefeated grace of God adopts us as His children.

2 & 3 John: The undefeated grace of God promised that the truth abides in us and will be with us forever.

Jude: The undefeated grace of God is found in the Christ who keeps us.

Revelation: The undefeated grace of God is seen in the revelation of the One who was and who is and who is to come, the One who is worthy to unroll the scroll, the One who is seated on the throne.[xli]

2. Give Grace to Your Spouse

God expects marriage to be the place where husband and wife exercise their grace muscles. Have you ever joined a 24-hour fitness club? *Anytime Fitness* was the first 24-hour gym I ever joined. I could go work out on any day at any time. It was great. Marriage grants you the opportunity to exercise your grace muscles 24/7. You can give grace to your spouse on any day and at any time.

Are you giving grace to your spouse? Or, are you with-holding grace from your spouse? Consider these questions from Greg Smalley:

- Do you become frustrated over little things your spouse does or doesn't do?

- Do certain quirks your spouse has irritate you?
- Are you tired of trying to change your spouse?
- Does your spouse accuse you of nitpicking?
- Do you lose your patience and snap at your spouse?
- Do you assume the worst about your spouse?
- Are you overly critical of your spouse?
- Do you expect your spouse to read your mind?

Grace is to be given, not withheld. According to Smalley, if you answered "yes" to these questions, then you are withholding grace from your spouse.[xlii]

Grace doesn't assume the worst but believes the best about your spouse. Grace moves you toward your spouse. Grace takes away the urge to get even with your spouse. Grace displays the gospel to your spouse. Grace should be given freely as it was freely given to you. Don't be like Mr. or Mrs. Law, but be like Mr. and Mrs. Grace.

> We were married to Mr. Law. He was a good man, in his way, but he did not understand our weakness. He came home every evening and asked, "So, how was your day? Did you do what I told you to? Did you make the kids behave? Did you waste any time? Did you complete everything I put on your To Do list?" So many demands and expectations. And hard as we tried, we couldn't be perfect. We could never satisfy him. We forgot things that were important to him. We let the children misbehave. We failed in other ways. It was a miserable marriage, because Mr. Law always pointed out our failings. And the worst

of it was, he was always right! But his remedy was always the same: Do better tomorrow. We didn't, because we couldn't.

Then Mr. Law died. And we remarried, this time to Mr. Grace. Our new husband, Jesus, comes home every even-ing and the house is a mess, the children are being naughty, dinner is burning on the stove, and we have even had other men in the house during the day. Still, he sweeps us into his arms and says, "I love you, I chose you, I died for you, I will never leave you nor forsake you." And our hearts melt. We don't understand such love. We expect him to despise us and reject us and humiliate us, but he treats us so well. We are so glad to belong to him now and forever, and we long to be "fully pleasing to him!"

Being married to Mr. Law never changed us. But being married to Mr. Grace is changing us deep within, and it shows.[xliii]

Critique your spouse gently and encourage your spouse fiercely.

No one gives grace better than a person who has been given grace. Give grace to your spouse. What does grace look like? Critique your spouse gently and encourage your spouse fiercely.

3. Gross Out Your Kids

As a dad of a fourteen-year-old and a twelve-year-old, it's my job to embarrass them as much as humanly possible. One of my favorite ways to do that is to kiss their momma. When I lay one on Tonya and I hear Braydee and Belle say, "Ew that's gross" it's music to my ears. If your children have never said "Ew that's gross" to you kissing or hugging your spouse, then you are doing it wrong! I constantly show and tell my girls that I am all about their momma. Husband and wife, your kids need to see that you are crazier about each other than you are about them. Remember, Jesus first, your spouse second, and the kids third. Kids third! Children will never feel more secure than knowing mom and dad can't get enough of each other. Show them by laying down the law that your love for your spouse comes before them.

When I was growing up...I know, that is so lame. The proverbial "when I was growing up we walked in the snow four miles uphill back and forth to school every day." Still, when I was growing up, the man of the house was the first one to eat. Children didn't eat first. Children waited while the adults ate. Right now, I am writing this chapter while we are on a mission trip with our church in St. Louis. Each night the team eats together for dinner and the first people in line are the little people. What happened? What changed? Parents worship their children. That's what happened. That's what changed. It's not the children's fault, it's the parent's fault. It's our fault, not their fault. Please don't forget, Jesus first, spouse second, and children third.

I promise you I love my girls, Braydee and Belle, and they know it. I just love their momma more, and they know it.

Oh, and another thing. Y'all, your kids got to get out of your bed! Get your kids out of your bedroom. Make it clear that your bedroom is off limits to the little people. The more you get them out of your bedroom the more you'll move your marriage from good to gooder to goodest to great! Get them out! I promise you I love my girls Braydee and Belle, and they know it. I just love their momma more, and they know it. Ed Young Jr. was teaching on the barriers to an intimate

GOSPEL CONVERSATIONAL MARRIAGE

sex life in marriage and said "kids" stands for *keeping intimacy at a distance successfully.*[xliv] Get the kids out of your bedroom!

4. Get to Laughing

Is laughter lacking in your home? Is laughter lacking in your marriage? Is everyone too angry to laugh? Do you know one of the best ways to become slow to anger? Get off social media. Now! Do you know one of the best ways to become slow to tweet, slow to post, slow to text, and slow to troll? Turn off your phone and tune in to your spouse. Do you know one of the best ways to tune in to your spouse? Stop tweeting about your spouse and start talking to your spouse. Don't post about your spouse more than you spend time making the most with your spouse.

You need to stop being so serious. Easier said than done, right? How can we not keep from being on pins and needles all the time in this cancel-everybody and anything- goes culture? We live in a political, racial, and social mess. How can we not be serious all the time? Laugh at yourself, laugh at one another, and laugh with one another. God has a sense of humor, just look in the mirror. God wants you to enjoy one another and enjoy Him. Since that is true, don't forget to have fun. Laugh.

5. Go Out of Your Way to Get Away

If you don't go out of your way to get away, then you will never get away. What does it take to go out of your way to get away? Intentionality. Be intentional. Be aware that you need to take care of your marriage. Plan a weekend away. Stop right now. Put this book down and pick up your calendar. Call your spouse and y'all plan a trip at this very minute. Get it on your calendar or it will never get on your calendar. I'll be here when you get back.

Connecting..............

Glad your back. Your marriage can be better on earth.

She Says

I love grace. I just can't get enough of it. I remember hearing about it for the first time in Mark and Peggy Hayman's Sunday school class. I was a brand-new Christian, and all I understood about God and Heaven was that I never knew from day to day if I'd been good enough to get there. I cried like a baby when Ephesians 2:8 & 9 were explained to me:

> *For by grace you have been saved through faith. And this is not your own doing; it is the gift of God, not a result of works, so that no one may boast. For we are his workmanship, created in Christ Jesus for good works, which God prepared beforehand, that we should walk in them.*

I cried like a baby in that Sunday school class. I know everyone else thought I was crazy. Most of them had been in that church all of their lives and already knew these things. I had gone to school with most of these young adults since this was my hometown. I was never good enough to be friends with them in school though (that's just the way I thought in those days), so I was incredibly intimidated and vulnerable by sobbing that day. But I couldn't help it. Those words SET ME FREE. No longer did I need to make sure my skirts went all the way down past my knees, no longer did it matter that I wore make up and jewelry or cut my hair. No longer would I go to bed at night wondering if I had done enough "good" to outweigh the "bad."

GOSPEL CONVERSATIONAL MARRIAGE

I recently posted about a time when I stuck my foot in my mouth. I do it all the time. I'm always putting myself out there so I frequently make a fool of myself. Yes, I take full advantage of that grace stuff. Gotta make up for lost time. But ya know what, God has my heart and I won't live in shame anymore.

I love to get to Sunday morning worship early so I can walk around and meet new faces. Rarely does this actually happen. I'm usually running in during the first song. But this one particular Sunday, I made it early to the worship center and was walking around, and I did it. My brain is often not my friend. I stuck my big ole Jessica Simpson encrusted foot right into my mouth. I introduced myself to a couple who have been members for 3 years! Yes, I did. Thankfully they were extremely gracious and laughed at me instead of making me feel like an idiot.

I desperately want to know everyone, and it's hard. I know many longtime members who are afraid to introduce themselves to new faces because they are afraid that they, too, are longtime members and it will hurt someone's feelings. I get that too. But if I reintroduce myself to people, it just means, "I don't know you well, but I want to." So, I'm sure that won't be the last time I do that. I'll keep pulling my Jessicas out of my mouth if that means I can connect with someone I don't know. But I'm so grateful for the ones who bestow me the extra grace. We all need more grace.

God freely gives us this grace so we need to freely give it to others. Does that mean we have to let others abuse us? No. We need healthy boundaries which is a whole other chapter. But I have defiantly cut malicious people out of my life. Doesn't mean I'm mad at them—even the malicious ones don't need that power over you—but you'd be a fool if you kept letting them into your life to abuse you.

When I see a couple who have been married for most of their lifetime, I see a couple who knows grace. I recently met a lady in the guest reception who came with a friend she had been best friends with for 50+ years! Wow! My best friend was also there, and I told her we'd been best friends since we'd come to this church. She brought tears to my eyes when she told me all of the dark things they had gone through together. One of the friends had lost a child and the other, her husband. We should all cherish lifelong friends. Us girls need girlfriends! Like marriages, it takes grace to have friends that long. Chances are, none of us will have a spouse or friend that long without needing gobs and gobs of grace.

Fellas, us girls tend to be emotional. Where guys live by facts and ambitions, we live by emotions and relationships. Emotions tend to swell on a dime for some of us, so just stay calm, let us have our moment, and then laugh with us about it when we are ready.

Notice how in a previous chapter I mentioned that in 23 years together, Sam has never raised his voice to ME? Notice how I didn't say I'd never raised my voice to HIM? Well, that's because I have a tendency to overreact. Yes, yes, I do. But Sam always manages to stay calm, lets me rant, and then we laugh about it later. We ALWAYS end up laughing about it. I know there are times when it seems there couldn't possibly be anything to laugh about, but I believe grace gives us the opportunity if we'll look for it. Life is always throwing hard things at us, but take heart—God is good and He's in control. My dad always says, "It ain't the end of the world, and even if it is, you won't be worried about X situation." This earth is not our home. We are just visitors here. Everything here is temporary, even when it seems like the end of the world.

And please extend grace to yourselves. Forgive yourself for missteps. It's not the end of the world. If there are things in the past you wish you'd done differently, try to fix it. If you can't, let it go. Don't let the past rule your future. If people have hurt you, let it go. It takes too much energy to be mad and disgruntled. Life is short, and God has given us a mission. We can't serve God and constantly lick our wounds. Put some essential oils on that wound, and let it heal up!

Now, go forgive your spouse (and kids and friends). Allow them to make mistakes. Allow them to be who God created them to be, and stop trying to make them into who you want them to be. Take full advantage of that grace stuff! What if we just gave away a small fraction of ALL the grace we have received? The world would be a different place, and your marriage would be much more fulfilling!

xoxo

Must Be the Shoes

Tonya likes shoes, but I like shoes more. Tonya has many shoes, but I have more shoes. Well, if you don't count flip flops, then I have more shoes. As an adult, Tonya has more flip flops than flips I flopped as a child. So, not counting flip flops I have more shoes than my wife. No grown man should ever own as many shoes as I own. Pray for me. Please. Paul wrote in Romans 10:14-15:

How then will they call on him in whom they have not believed? And how are they to believe in him of whom they have never heard? And how are they to hear without someone preaching? And how are they to preach unless they are sent? As it is written, How beautiful are the feet of those who preach the good news!

Of all the shoes I own, Tonya and I can both attest that there is nothing beautiful about my feet. Feet bring forth many thoughts. Feet make us say "gross"! Feet stink. Feet swell. Feet look funny. Feet hurt. Feet may cause us to think about many things, but beauty is not the first thing we associate with feet. Paul was writing about the feet attached to people who come to tell good news. Feet that are attached to people who are spreading the gospel of Jesus Christ are beautiful in the sight of God. Converse are my favorite shoes because they remind me that I am a gospel conversationalist sent by Jesus to engage people in gospel conversations.

Think about all those nasty feet Jesus washed as He spent time washing His disciples' feet. Jesus washed dirty feet (Judas), unbelieving feet (Thomas), insert-foot-in-mouth feet (Peter), worn out feet (John), wounded feet (James), dragging feet (Nathaniel), and tired feet (Andrew). In John 13:4-5, 14 the Bible says:

He laid aside his outer garments, and taking a towel, tied it around his waist. Then he poured water into a basin and began to wash the disciples' feet and to wipe them with the towel that was wrapped around him...If I then, your Lord and Teacher, have washed your feet, you also ought to wash one another's feet.

Feet in the first century Jewish context were always nasty and dirty because people wore sandals and the roadways were dusty. Basins to wash feet were present at the front door of nearly every home. Foot washing was reserved for slaves only. Masters would NEVER wash anyone's feet. For a Master (Jesus) to wash His servants' (disciples) yucky, dirty, icky, and dusty feet was unheard of, uncalled for, and never done. Enter Jesus. Jesus did things differently. He was teaching His followers about a different kingdom. The disciples needed their feet washed first and then they could wash one another's feet.

Husbands and wives, you need Jesus to give you a spiritual foot washing. Perhaps you or your spouse has spiritually dirty feet, spiritually tired feet, spiritually wounded feet, or maybe you're spiritually dragging your feet. You can't change your spouse. Stop trying. Your spouse can't change you. Stop looking to him or her as the one who can change you. Only Jesus can spiritually wash your feet. Which feet represent you?

Dirty Feet. Jesus told His disciples that not all of them were clean. Judas was not spiritually clean. Some of you have spiritually dirty feet. Only Christ can clean you from all your sin and make you acceptable to a holy God. You must put God first. Yes, even before your spouse. If your relationship with Jesus is wrong, then your relationship with your spouse will never be right. Ask Jesus to make you clean. Repent and believe in Jesus.

Tired feet. Some of you are serving your spouse well, but you are tired. You are tired of serving and not being served in return. You are doing all the giving and your spouse is doing all the taking. You are worn out. Ask the Holy Spirit to give you the strength to continue to serve well. Serve in the power of the Holy Spirit.

Dragging your feet. Some of you are dragging your feet. You are not serving your spouse. You are not serving your church. You are taking and not giving. Ask the Holy Spirit to give you a servant's heart.

Wounded feet. Abused people abuse people. Hurting people hurt people. Wounded people wound people. Your wounded spouse has wounded you. You are hurting. Jesus can heal you and your marriage. Ask Him.[xlv]

What She Needs Is Not What He Needs

The battle of the blinds is an everyday battle at the Greer house. When I get home each day from work, I close the blinds. On weekdays I leave the house earlier than the girls get up. So, when Tonya rises in the mornings, she opens the blinds. I close the blinds. Tonya opens the blinds. Tonya likes the sun. I am allergic to the sun. What Tonya likes and what I like aren't always alike, and that's alright.

Tonya says "Yum!" to mayonnaise, while I say "Yuck!" I say "Yum!" to onions, while Tonya says "Yuck!" Tonya says "Yum!" to coffee, while I say "Yuck!" (Nothing on earth smells better and at the same time tastes worse than coffee. Come at me.) I say "Yum!" to shrimp, while Tonya says "Yuck to all the ways that Bubba Gump can prepare shrimp!" Tonya says "Yum!" to Greek yogurt, while I say "Yuck, that is Greek to me!" I say "Yay!" to sports, while Tonya says "No way!" Tonya says "I love lamp" to lamps, I say "I hate lamp." In a similar way that you and your spouses' preferences differ, your needs differ.

What Tonya likes and what I like aren't always alike, and that's alright.

What she needs is not what he needs, and what he needs is not what she needs. Have you considered your spouses' needs? How are you going to serve your spouse (wash his or her feet) if you don't know what he or she needs? William F. Harley, in his popular book, *His Needs, Her Needs,* identifies the ten most important needs of men and women. He offers five needs for her and five for him.

1. She needs affection.

2. He needs sexual fulfillment.

3. She needs conversation.

4. He needs recreational companionship.

5. She needs honesty and openness.

6. He needs an attractive spouse.

7. She needs financial support.

8. He needs domestic support.

9. She needs family commitment.

10. He needs admiration.[xlvi]

Have you considered your spouses' needs? How are you going to serve your spouse (wash his or her feet) if you don't know what he or she needs?

Knowing your spouse's needs is half the battle when it comes to meeting those needs. Husbands and wives, your spouse should never be looking to have his or her needs fulfilled outside of your marriage. Don't give him or her a reason to look elsewhere. Meet your spouse's needs!

Will You Still Be Married in Heaven?

Prior to answering the call to vocational ministry, I worked as a financial planner. We had a strong team at the firm where I worked. One of those guys was Justin. He enjoyed the spotlight and did well as a financial planner. Justin and his wife Carmen became good friends of ours. Tonya and I even traveled with them on a vacation cruise. On the way down to the Florida port, we ran out of gas on the interstate. Running out of gas with another couple is an effective way to really get to know each other. And so, we did. Justin and I talked about faith quite a bit. We even talked about heaven. He was interested in knowing if He and Carmen would still be married in heaven. He said:

"If I am not married to Carmen in Heaven, then I don't want to go to Heaven."

Wow! I guess that is better than saying:

"If I am married to Carmen in Heaven, then I don't want to go to Heaven."

Will there be marriage in Heaven? Will we still be married in Heaven? Spouses who are saved will be reunited with one another in Heaven, but they will not be married. In Luke 20:34-36, Jesus said:

The sons of this age marry and are given in marriage, but those who are considered worthy to attain to that age and to the resurrection from the dead neither marry nor are given in marriage, for they cannot die anymore, because they are equal to angels and are sons of God, being sons of the resurrection.

Jesus made it clear that in Heaven we will not still be married to our spouse. Why?

First, the very nature of life after death is nothing like life before death. The world to come is totally different than the world now here. The new heavens and the new earth will be on a whole new level than the current heavens and earth. Second, marriage on earth serves the purpose of protection against sin, procreation to fill the hole death leaves, and to be a reflection of Christ and His church. In Heaven all three of these purposes are eliminated. We need no reflection because we see fully. Also, temptation, sin, and death are no more.[xlvii]

No, you won't be married to your spouse in Heaven. No, God is not being mean to you. The Bible says in 1 Corinthians 13:13:

So now faith, hope, and love abide, these three; but the greatest of these is love.

Hope is a confident assurance of what is to come. Faith is the assurance of things not yet seen. Both of these are unnecessary in Heaven. We won't need faith and hope in Heaven. Love is the greatest because it is the only one remaining in Heaven. Marriage was designed by God to make us holy, not happy. Holiness, preparing us for Heaven, is one of the purposes of marriage. Once we make it to Heaven, marriage is no longer needed between spouses.

At the time that Justin made that bold statement of not wanting to go to Heaven unless he and Carmen were still married, they had a great marriage. It's always better to have a good marriage than a bad marriage. Justin verbalized what many people internalize. He said what we have all thought. Since having a good marriage is the best of the best on earth, then how is Heaven without the institution of marriage far better? How is Heaven without your marriage far better?

Heaven Without Your Marriage Is Still Far Better

Do you believe God? I am not asking if you believe in God, but do you believe God? In reality, people who claim to be atheist may doubt God's promises more than God's presence. That is, they may not necessarily doubt the existence of God, but they may doubt more the extensiveness of God. How can you not believe in the existence of the Creator God? A human being giving birth to another human being is evidence enough in the existence of God. A sunset or sunrise is proof enough in the existence of God. I am convinced that it is much easier to believe in God, the existence of God, than to believe God. Do you believe God? Do you believe God's Word? Do you believe in the promises of God? Do you believe what God has said about marriage? Do you believe what God has said about Heaven?

What has God said about marriage? Marriage is a covenant relationship between one man and one woman for a lifetime. God has said that what He brought together man shall not separate. God's design for marriage is that two become one flesh. God's design for marriage is non-negotiable.

What has God said about heaven? In Philippians 1:23, Paul wrote:

My desire is to depart and be with Christ, for that is far better.

Paul believed God so much that his very desire was to leave this earth and go be with Jesus in Heaven. Wow!

Few people are guilty of saying,

"I am ready to die and go to Heaven right now!"

Most sane people will say,

"I want to go to Heaven."

Far less, if any, will say,

"I want to go to Heaven right now."

Paul was saying,

"I want to go to Heaven right now! My desire is to go, right now, and be with Jesus in Heaven!"

Why do we not desire the same? I'll tell you why. We DO NOT believe God. We don't! When it comes to not believing God, we must admit it and quit it! Paul believed that heaven really is far better than any experience on this earth. So should we.

Churches are full of folks who are practical atheists. Practical atheists are those whose lips say they believe God, but their life says differently. The satirical website *The Babylon Bee* posted an article entitled: "New Atheist Chick-fil-A Competitor Only Open on Sundays."

The article read:

"Militant atheist Carl Burke has made a new restaurant chain called Chick-fil-Atheist that is *only* open on Sundays in defiance of God and Christian worship."[xlviii]

Just like the Chick-fil-Atheist only being open on Sundays, practical atheists live as if God is only God on Sundays. Too many in the church and in marriages behave as if what God says only applies on Sundays.

Don't be a practical atheist. Don't be a Chick-fil-Atheist. Believe God every day, not just on Sundays. Believe God when His Word says that Heaven is far better. Take any and every relationship and experience on earth, and it will be far better in Heaven. Even marriage relationships and experiences are far better in Heaven. God gave husbands and wives sex in marriage to enjoy and it is enjoyable. In Heaven, we will not have sex, but there will be something far better. Imagine that! The best day, moment, or experience you've ever had in your marriage pales in comparison to what Heaven will be like.

Marriage Supper of the Lamb

No, you will not still be married in Heaven. Yes, you will know your spouse in Heaven even more than you know him or her on earth. Though there will not be any marriages from earth in Heaven, there is one marriage in Heaven.

Due to *death do us part*, all marriages end in separation, except one.

All earthly marriages end at death. Marriage on earth is meant to last a lifetime. Marriage on earth is meant to last until *death do us part*. Because of death, even marriages that last a lifetime end in separation. That's right, due to *death do us part*, all marriages end in separation, except one. In Revelation 19:9, the Bible says:

> And the angel said to me, "Write this: Blessed are those who are invited to the marriage supper of the Lamb."

What phase of a Jewish wedding celebration is the marriage supper? A first century Jewish wedding normally included three stages: (1) legal consummation of the marriage by the parents of the bride and the groom with the payment of the dowry, (2) the bridegroom coming to claim his bride, and (3) the wedding supper as seen in John 2:1-11. Revelation 19:9, *the wedding supper*, is stage three of a Jewish wedding in Jesus' day, but the wedding has yet to take place. The invitation is still being extended for all those who will accept. Husbands, Jesus is inviting you and your bride to be a part of His bride, the church. Have y'all accepted His invitation?

Do you and your spouse enjoy attending weddings? At most of the weddings Tonya and I attend, we don't get to sit together because I am the officiate. At the marriage supper of the Lamb, both Tonya and I will be a part of the bride of Christ. Jesus invites the uninvited to come. Our God is an inviting God. Jesus' desire is to have you as a part of His bride at the marriage supper of the Lamb.

Gonna Party Like It's Revelation 19:9

On October 27, 1982, American recording artist Prince released a song entitled *1999*. Part of the chorus reads, "So tonight I'm gonna party like it's 1999."[xlix] New Orleans Theological Seminary professor and AVP of Academic Affairs, Rhyne Putman, entitled a sermon "Gonna Party Like its Revelation 19:9." I like Rhyne's sermon title better than Prince's song title. Husbands and wives, why are we not waiting, serving, loving, witnessing, discipling, sharing, and partying like its Revelation 19:9?

During their wedding day photos, Clayton and Brittany Cook from Ontario, Canada, noticed three children following them around cheering & pointing at their wedding outfits. The couple was having wedding day photos taken near a body of water in Cambridge, Ontario. The groom kept a close eye on the young boys because they were getting really close to the water. Suddenly, the groom noticed that only two boys were standing near the water as one of the boys was in the water struggling to keep his head above the water. While his bride was having some solo photos taken, the groom jumped from the park bridge into the water and saved the little boy from drowning. Of her groom, the bride said, "He's my hero!"

Marriage on earth should be an ongoing praise party as husband and wife look forward to the marriage in Heaven found in Revelation 19:9.

Can you imagine how much sweeter the celebration was at that wedding in Ontario, Canada after the groom saved that little boy? Little girls grow up dreaming about their future groom being their hero. Jesus, the bridegroom, has jumped off heaven's eternal bridge into the sinful waters of this earth to save you from drowning in your sin. Jesus is our hero! Marriage on earth should be an ongoing praise party as husband and wife look forward to the marriage in Heaven found in Revelation 19:9.

Before you read the next chapter, have an impromptu dance party right now! Go! Dance!

SAM & TONYA GREER

CONVERSATION STARTERS

1. Read Ephesians 2:8-10. What is your understanding of grace? Discuss with your spouse.

2. In what way has your spouse recently given you grace? Go tell him or her about that specific time, what it meant to you, and thank him or her for being gracious to you.

3. Talk about showing your children God is first, mom and dad second, and they're third. Make a plan to do this.

4. In what ways could you and your spouse better meet one another's needs? Discuss

Conversation 8

In Sickness…

There was a man in the land of Uz whose name was Job and that man was blameless and upright, one who feared God and turned away from evil.
Job 1:1

Are you expecting the unexpected? What happens when bad things happen in marriage? Why do bad things happen to good people in marriage?

Are You Expecting the Unexpected?

Sometimes the unexpected happens. I didn't see it coming. We all have personal preferences and pet peeves. One of my pet peeves is seeing able-bodied people who are riding on those motorized Walmart carts. You know, the cart with the basket on the front, the handlebar behind the basket, running boards on the bottom for your feet, and a seat on the back of the cart. I am more apt to sit on the judgment seat when I see an able-bodied person sitting on a Walmart motorized cart seat. As long as I am able, I have vowed never to sit on a motorized Walmart cart seat.

SAM & TONYA GREER

As I pulled into the Walmart Neighborhood Market parking lot, I saw a sweet little elderly lady wrestling to unload her groceries from her Walmart motorized cart. Clearly, this lady was a perfect, legit candidate for the usage of a motorized cart. She had her walking cane in the basket, and she was struggling to pivot from the cart to put her groceries in her car. At one point I just knew she was about to fall.

Racing across the parking lot to help her, I asked,

"Ma'am, may I help you with your groceries?"

She responded,

"No, thank you, I just loaded the last bag."

I reached over into the basket and took her walking cane and handed it to her. Then, she said,

"Well, you could help me by returning this cart back into the store so I don't have to make the trip."

How could I say no to that?

"Yes ma'am!" She sincerely said, "Thank you."

There I was standing next to this cart. I have one hand on the handlebars and one hand on the back of the seat trying to push the cart. It won't budge. I begin to think to myself,

"Is the battery dead? No. Will it go forward? No. Will it go back-ward? No."

I tried pushing it forward and backward to no avail. For one to two minutes I am trying to get this cart to move. Yet, this cart is having no part of moving.

By this time, the sweet elderly lady has made her way back around the car and said,

"Are you having trouble?"

In a tone of frustration, I blurted out,

"I can't get this cart to move."

With a look only a grandmother could give, she said,

"Oh, son, the cart won't move unless you are sitting on the seat. You have to sit on the seat for it to move."

Me? Sit on this seat? No way! At this point, I decided, I am going to wait until she drives off, and I will go get a Walmart employee to get the cart.

Then, looking directly at me, the lady said,

"Now, I am going to stand here and not leave until you return that cart back into the store. Someone else may need to use it."

I reluctantly said,

"Yes ma'am."

I, an able-bodied grown man, sat down on that Walmart motorized cart and drove it through the parking lot back to the store. The speed of that cart was slower than Blobby the Blob's motorized scooter in *Hotel Transylvania 2*. I had one foot on the ground trying to kick it along. All the while, people were driving by staring at me, judging me. By the way, I don't judge them for judging me. In fact, I would have judged me, too.

Upon arriving at the front of the store, I noticed a Walmart employee standing outside the store on her break. I said to her,

"I am returning this cart for an elderly lady."

The employee, not believing a word I said, looked at me and gave me an,

"Mmmm. Hmmm. You are too kind."

Sometimes the unexpected happens. What happens when the unexpected, like driving a motorized cart, is more than just a humiliating and crushing blow to your pride? What happens when the unexpected is outright bad? What happens when bad things happen?

What Happens When Bad Things Happen?

Job had one job. His sole job was to worship God. Even when Job's world fell apart, he took his job of worshiping God seriously. Job was a good steward of his suffering. What can we learn from Job stewarding his suffering well? How can we steward our suffering well?

Our plans may be pure. First, we need to know that in marriage our plans may be pure, we may play our cards right, and we may believe and behave right, but suffering still surfaces. Job was a righteous man living a righteous life. As a person, a parent, and a public figure, Job played his cards right for he was upright. In Ezekiel 14:13-14, the Bible says:

GOSPEL CONVERSATIONAL MARRIAGE

Son of man, when a land sins against me by acting faithlessly, and I stretch out my hand against it and break its supply of bread and send famine upon it, and cut off from it man and beast, even if these three men, Noah, Daniel, and Job, were in it, they would deliver but their own lives by their righteousness, declares the LORD God.

Noah was the only righteous man living during his day. Daniel remained righteous before God and faithful to God while in Babylon. Job was the greatest of all the people of the East in his day. He wasn't merely a wise man from the East; rather, he was the wisest of the wisest from the East. Job turned away from evil and turned to the LORD. He gathered his children to worship once a week. Job's plans were pure, but suffering still surfaced.

Our plans were pure. Tonya and I heard God's call on our life, and we left the life that we knew. We left our life of living close to everyone we loved, everyone we knew, and everything that was comfortable. It was hard to do, but God blessed us all the way through. We sold what we had and moved to Slidell, Louisiana to start seminary at New Orleans Baptist Theological Seminary (NOBTS). Our plan was to live on the campus, but there was one problem. NOBTS didn't then nor does it now allow Corona, not the virus, on campus. We learned early in the application process that the policy of NOBTS was *no Corona on campus*. See, God asked Tonya to leave her mom, dad, brother, home, church, small group, friends, job, and more. I was not about to ask Tonya to leave her Corona. So, we found an apartment in Slidell that would allow us to have Corona. We left everything behind except for Tonya's Corona. I guess now would be a good time to inform you that Corona was our two-pound Chihuahua. What else would you've associated with Corona? I mean, come on, we are Southern Baptist! How did Corona get her name? Alright, I'll tell you. Corona was already named when she was given to us. You do believe that, right?

Our plan to follow wherever God called us to go was pure. I am so frustrated with pastors who want to take the elevator in ministry and not the stairs. The majority of us pastors don't start as the pastor of a large church. Pastors, you need to obey God and go where God tells you to go or stay where He tells you to stay. I can remember hearing at a pastor's conference some years ago,

"Every pastor needs to be fired by a church once."

What does that mean? The speaker was not referring to pastors being fired for moral failures. He was saying that pastors need to be willing to go to the hard churches. If there are any easy churches in existence, they're all taken. Tonya and I weren't looking to make it big, build our kingdom, or get rich in ministry. We just wanted to follow wherever God led. We just didn't anticipate or realize that God would lead us right into suffering.

Our perspective is partial. If you have ever read Job, then you were probably struck by the reality that Job had no idea what was going on behind the scenes. Satan accused God. Satan accused Job. News flash—*If Satan accused God and Job, then he is accusing you and your spouse.* The good news is that Satan answers to God. Tony Evans said:

> If all you see is what you see, then you don't see all there is to be seen.[1]

God is working not only behind the scenes but also behind the *seen*. God sees all. Nothing has happened, happens, or will happen outside of God's sight. As Job saw his suffering increase, he had no idea what was happening behind the *seen*. Job 1:12,14-19 records much of Job's suffering:

And the LORD said of Satan, "Behold, all that he has is in your hand. Only against him do not stretch out your hand. So Satan went out from the presence of the LORD...and there came a messenger to Job and said, "The oxen were plowing and the donkeys feeding beside them, and the Sabeans fell upon them and took them and struck down the servants with the edge of the sword, and I alone have escaped to tell you." While he was speaking, there came another and said, "The fire of God fell from heaven and burned up the sheep and the servants and consumed them, and I alone have escaped to tell you." While he was yet speaking, there came another and said, "The Chaldeans formed three groups and made a raid on the camels and took them and struck down the servants with the edge of the sword, and I alone have escaped to tell you." While he was yet speaking, there came another and said, "Your sons and daughters were eating and drinking wine in their oldest brother's house, and behold, a great wind came across the wilderness and struck the four corners of the house, and it fell upon the young people, and they are dead, and I alone have escaped to tell you."

From Job's perspective, his world was falling apart. From God's perspective, the world was falling into place.

Our perspective was partial. The move to seminary required that Tonya and I quit our jobs and put our house up for sale. Get this! We went from having two jobs and paying for one place to live to having no jobs and paying for two places to live. Our income disappeared and our liabilities doubled: (1) two power bills, (2) two water bills, and (3) two housing bills (our apartment in Louisiana and our home in Mississippi). The ones closest to us thought we were crazy. But God. After two months of having no income and double the bills, God moved. On a trip home to Mississippi, I was able to give a testimony about what God was doing in our life at our home church. I asked the folks to pray that our home would sell. After the worship service, a man and his wife walked up and said, "We need to come see your house." God told them that, although they had already put an offer down on another house, they needed to come look at our house. Later that day they came to our house and made an offer. Five days later, we closed on the house. The very next Friday we came back to Mississippi for the closing of our house. Only God can move a house from being under contract on Sunday and closed five days later. We only and always see in part, not the whole.

Our pain has purpose. Don't you wish you could silence Satan? Don't you wish there was a Zoom and doom mute button you could push to silence Satan? Your worship of God in the midst of suffering silences Satan. When you are struck by suffering and you still worship God through the suffering, Satan can only be silent. Job's suffering silenced Satan. Do you realize that your suffering can shut Satan up? Satan accused Job of only worshiping God because God had blessed Job. In fact, Satan argued that if God would allow Job to suffer, then Job would curse God. Well, did Job curse God? Job's response to his suffering is found in Job 1:20-22:

Then Job arose and tore his robe and shaved his head and fell on the ground and worshiped. And he said, "Naked I came from my mother's womb, and naked shall I return. The LORD gave, and the LORD has taken away; Blessed be the name of the LORD." In all this Job did not sin or charge God with wrong.

Job didn't curse God, but worshiped God. The most effective way for you to silence Satan is to worship God.

Sure, Satan is heard around the world more than Siri. I know it feels like Satan will never be silenced. I know you feel like you are at the end of your rope, and you can't take one more disappointment. You can't take one more word of bad news. You can't handle one more bad phone call. You can't take one more surprise. Remember this, our disappointments are God's appointments. Our pain has purpose. God doesn't waste your suffering. God doesn't waste your pain. God may not always calm your storm, but He will always be your calm in the storm. Worship Him!

This is Uz

This is Us is one of the most popular TV shows in recent years. In the article, "Why is 'This is Us' so popular? The answer is simple," Gerald McRaney said:

'This is Us' is a success because it *IS* us![li]

Job 1:1 reads this way,

There was a man in the land of Uz, whose name was Job.

Job was not from the land of Oz. He was not from some make-believe land that Dorothy, The Tin Man, Scarecrow, and The Cowardly Lion visited. Dad joke alert: Why is the wizard of Oz the ultimate chick flick? Because it's a movie where two women are trying to kill each other over a pair of shoes. Sorry, I know that was terrible. Job was not from the land of Oz. Job was not from the land of Pez. One of my go-to candies growing up was Pez candy. I never could get that Pez dispenser loaded properly. You know what I mean? You ever tried to get the candy to load vertically, then it would turn horizontally and jam the dispenser up. At that point, I would just eat the whole pack of candy and forget the Pez dispenser. Job was not from the land of Oz (make believe) or the land of Pez (happy-go-lucky), but Job was from the land of Uz. The land of Uz represents lands of suffering. The land of Uz *IS* the land of us. This is Uz. Whether it be physical, emotional, spiritual, relational, or psychological, many marriages are living in the land of Uz. Tonya and I have lived in the land of Uz.

The land of Uz represents lands of suffering. The land of Uz *IS* the land of us. This is Uz.

When Tonya and I were standing on the beach in Maui, Hawaii, reciting our wedding vows, *in sickness and in health,* we never dreamed of any sickness. At twenty-seven and twenty-four years old, we were only thinking about health. After working so hard to lose over one-hundred and twenty pounds in my twenties, I ashamedly admit that my attitude about health was unhealthy. No mercy or compassion for people who were overweight or unhealthy. Put down the fork, and go work it off! I know that is terrible. Terrible. Tonya and I were living in the *play your cards right and you can somehow avoid suffering* camp. If we obey God, treat others well, don't cheat, work hard, try harder, walk the straight and narrow, and keep our nose clean, then we can escape suffering. So naïve. We simply thought that sickness only happens to those other people, but it would never happen to us. Sickness only happens to people who don't take care of themselves. We arrogantly believed if we ate right and exercised, then sickness would never be added unto us. We erroneously thought sickness happens to the weak, but not the strong. Oh, we couldn't have been more wrong.

Sixteen years after our wedding day, *that day* came. Oh, how I will never forget *that day*. Do you remember *that day*? You know, *that day* you were called into your boss' office and told you were no longer employed. *That day* you received the divorce papers. *That day* the phone call came that your loved one died. *That day* when your world fell apart. *That day* when life as you knew it was gone. Do you remember *that day*? In Job 1:13, the Bible says:

Now there was a day...

That day was a day Job never forgot. For Tonya and I, *that day* was the day we walked into the doctor's office. Like any other doctor's office on any day of the week, the waiting room was full of patients waiting to see the doctor. When we walked into the office, I was checking out what magazine might entertain for the next couple of hours.

As soon as the nurse saw us, she went back to get the doctor, and something happened that I have never experienced before and hope I never will again.

The doctor walked out into the waiting room straight toward us and said,

"Y'all come with me."

We followed the doctor back to the second waiting room. You do know about the second waiting room, right? The waiting room behind the waiting room where you are normally left waiting again. Well, we didn't even have to wait in the second waiting room.

The doctor walked in, closed the door, and said:

"Tonya, it's cancer."

I didn't hear anything else. I was stunned.

I used to be the person who would moan, groan and complain about waiting in a doctor's office waiting room. But, now, I am the person who can't wait to wait in the doctor's waiting room, because the alternative is devastating.

In April of 2017, Tonya was diagnosed with a rare form of cancer known as appendiceal and peritoneal carcinoma. In August of that same year, she underwent a long and intrusive Hyperthermic Intraperitoneal Chemotherapy (HIPEC) surgery. Part of the surgery included bathing Tonya's intestines in heated chemo. In addition, her surgeon removed every organ that wasn't vital and reconstructed Tonya intestines. Her surgery lasted over thirteen hours and was successful, but recovery was brutal as more surgeries were required. Ultimately, God healed Tonya. Praise the Lord she remains cancer free.

SAM & TONYA GREER

I have heard it said,

"I don't see how anybody makes it through life's trouble without Jesus."

I amen that twice: Amen! Amen! Yet, I would also say,

"I don't see how anybody makes it through life's trouble without Jesus' church."

Team Tonya became the slogan for Tonya's cancer battle, and we are appreciative for all who joined the team. Though forever thankful, we will never be able to thank our church family at Red Bank Baptist Church enough for all the prayers, support, food (especially the food), cards, acts of service, and so much more. So many churches from Chattanooga and beyond prayed for Tonya and supported us in ways we could never think or imagine.

The first time Tonya sat up in that hospital room chair after surgery was a hard but special day. She was in so much pain. I remember how long it took to do the simplest of tasks. Getting her legs and feet reclined in the chair was a chore. Then, putting a pair of wonder woman socks on her feet, that someone sent to her, felt like a Justice League victory. As we got her settled in the chair, I was able to do something for my wife I will never forget. Brush her hair. Y'all, my wife is a gorgeous woman. Don't get me wrong she is a beautiful woman on the inside, but she is a H.O.T. HOT! She takes really good care of herself and always looks her best. I knew she would want no hair out of place. Seeing Tonya suffer was hard, but there were moments, (like the times I got to brush her hair) that were sweet. Not so much for her, but oh so sweet for me. What a blessing!

In the midst of suffering, there were some sweet times, but there were also some not-so-sweet times. It was one of those long hospital days. Tonya just couldn't get comfortable as she tossed and turned. Nurses in and out of the room every hour. Beep! Beep! Beep!

GOSPEL CONVERSATIONAL MARRIAGE

Constant beeping from all the machines. Make. Them. Stop. I was standing at the foot of the bed trying to help Tonya get somewhat comfortable. She was frustrated, tired, hurting, medicated, and tired of me standing over her. With her feet sticking out from the covers, she looked at me and sternly said:

"You don't have to treat me like a child!"

Without missing a beat and in the same breadth, she said:

"Aren't you going to cover up my feet!?"

Stop treating me like a child! Are you going to stand there or cover up my feet? Once she recovered, Tonya and I had a belly laugh over that moment.

During Tonya's time of suffering, some moments were sweet, some were not-so-sweet, and some were scarier than seeing Jason Vorhees at a campfire. After Tonya's third surgery, she was unable to eat food and keep it down. A feeding tube was switched out each day by her nurse. Strict rules in the hospital called for me to keep my hands off of her feeding tube. Hands off! Don't come near it! Though I was her caregiver, touching that feeding tube meant that I would need care after being beatdown by Tonya's nurse. Feeding tubes are dangerous for people with no training to handle. Hands off! One wrong move with that feeding tube and Tonya could get an infection or worse. Alright, I got it. Hands off the feeding tube!

On the day that Tonya was being released from the hospital, I felt like I woke up in the Twilight Zone. Her nurse and doctor sent us home with the feeding tube. That conversation when something like this:

"Sam, we are sending you home to administer the feeding tube each day and night."

With a look of fear and bewilderment, I replied:

"What? You told me I was not allowed to touch the feeding tube and now I am in charge of giving it to her each day?"

Tonya's nurse replied:

"We will send you home with an instructional video for the usage of the feeding tube."

Shocked and confused, I said:

"You are going to send us home with an instructional video? That seems irresponsible and dangerous."

As she was walking out of the room, the nurse turned around and in an I-almost-forgot like gesture, said:

"Oh yeah, due to copyright laws and the risk of our competitors attaining the video, you will only be able to watch the video once. One viewing is all that is allowed."

Scared as a cat in a room full of rocking chairs, I said:

"Who am I Ethan Hunt on an impossible mission? This video message will self-destruct in ten seconds."

Each week more boxes were delivered to our house filled with feeding tubes, bags of liquid food, and all the equipment needed to administer. I was terrified. One mistake and Tonya would be in dire straits.

A Helpless Helper

Caregiving is a blessing and a curse. I was blessed to be able to care for Tonya at a time when she couldn't care for herself. It was also a curse because I couldn't make it better. I just wanted to make it better. I just wanted to fix the situation. Before the feeding tube, I tried to find something that Tonya would eat. She couldn't keep anything down. She tried soup, slushies, smoothies, and milkshakes; nothing worked. She lost so much weight. I was worried and frustrated because I couldn't make her better. You ever feel like you're no help at all. For much of Tonya's sickness, I felt like a helpless helper. I could do nothing to make it better. I could do nothing to make the pain go away. It was so hard watching her in so much pain and growing weaker. Suffering sucks. It can suck the happiness out of your life, it can suck the life out of your marriage, and it can suck the joy out of your salvation. What did I learn from being a helpless helper?

Pray, even when you don't feel like it. One rough day when Tonya was sick and I wanted to pray over her, she told me:

"I don't feel like praying."

So real. So raw. So true. Watching your spouse suffer will teach you to pray without ceasing. Pray for relief. Pray for healing. Pray for strength for yourself as you care for your spouse. Ask other people to pray specifically for you as you care for your spouse. When it comes to praying, Satan can't stop God from answering, but Satan can stop you from asking. Don't stop asking. The only unanswered prayers are unasked prayers. God's answer to prayer may not be your answer, but God answers. God always heals. It's just a matter of when and where.

Be patient with your patient. Caring for a spouse who is suffering takes patience. The good news is that patience can be learned. You can learn patience. The bad news is that patience must be learned. You must learn patience. We are called to bear with one another, that is, to put up with one another. Your spouse should be the first person you bear with in love. THAT is patience. Think about how patient God has been with you. Don't you imagine that He can give you and your spouse the patience to bear with one another. Yes. He. Can.

Rely on God. I still can't get over it! It's just leaves this Baptist preacher almost speechless, almost. That is saying something. I can't get over the fact that God doesn't need us, but He wants us. Meanwhile, we don't want God, but we need Him. Never live your life as if you don't need God. You need God. Yes, there are times when your need for God seems greater than other times and vice versa. But the truth is we always need God. Times of suffering for either you or your spouse will remind you that God will give you more than you can handle, but He will never give you more than He can handle. Lean into the Lord. Go with God. Just trust Jesus.

Reach out. Doctors need doctors. Dentists need dentists. Teachers need teachers. Pastors need pastors. Caregivers need caregivers. You can't give yourself the care that you need. When your spouse is suffering, you can give your spouse the care that he or she needs, but due to his or her suffering your spouse may be unable to reciprocate. Make sure that you are taking care of yourself as well as your spouse. I recently flew on a commercial airline and discovered a new level of human stupidity. During the airline safety instructions, a flight attendant spoke over the intercom system and said:

"Be sure to remove your COVID-19 surgical mask before putting on your oxygen mask."

C'mon! Really? Is this where we are as a society? Is this our level of intellect? Common sense is so uncommon. Just as airline safety protocol calls for securing one's own oxygen mask before helping someone else, make sure you are getting the care you need as a caregiver. Reach out.

You are making a difference. Don't buy into the lie that you are not making a difference as you care for your spouse? Even if that means days of sitting in silence with your spouse, you are making a difference. Your family is watching, your friends are watching, your church is watching, other married couples are watching, and those who are of the world are watching. A dear friend of mine has been caring for his wife for years. He is making a difference because he is not indifferent toward his calling to be different. Jesus is making a difference through you.

Don't be too hard on yourself. Give yourself a break. Caregiving is no easy job, just ask Job's wife. In Job 2:9-10, Job's wife was having a bad day:

Then his wife said to him, 'Do you still hold fast your integrity? Curse God and die.' But he said to her, 'You speak as one of the foolish women would speak. Shall we receive good from God, and shall we not receive evil?' In all this Job did not sin with his lips.

Of all the things God allowed Satan to take from Job, He didn't allow Satan to take Job's wife. Or, did He? God told Satan in Job 2:6:

'Behold, he [Job] is in your hand; only spare his life.'

Maybe Satan was bad of hearing and thought God said *only spare his wife*, not *life*. In the heat of this difficult marriage moment, Job may have thought *God, my suffering would be better if you had not spared my wife.* The Bible only says that Job didn't sin with his *lips,* but what about his *thoughts*? Ladies, I am joking! But caregiving in marriage is no joke. It's hard on the patient and the one administer-ing the care.

One of the lowest days of Tonya's suffering happened while in the hospital. Tonya was exhausted. I was exhausted. We had been in the hospital together for weeks. I hadn't slept in days. I remember Tonya needing to get up and walk around but I was in and out of sleep. I was no help. She had to get the nurse to come get her out of bed and walk around the halls of the hospital. When I woke up, she tore into me. She told me to leave the hospital. Get out. She told me that she knew I didn't want to be with her anyway. It was hard to hear, but deep down I knew it wasn't Tonya speaking. It was the medication, the grief, the pain, the suffering, and the hurt speaking. Though it still hurt, I was stubborn enough to stay. Don't beat yourself up caregivers. At least you have not responded to your spouse's suffering like Job's wife. And if you have, just be stubborn enough to stay.

Don't be too hard on others. Suffering changes how a person is seen. In Isaiah 52:14, the Bible speaks to Messiah's suffering:

As many were astonished at you—his appearance was so marred, beyond human semblance, and his form beyond that of the children of mankind.

Jesus became flesh and dwelt among us. He was not created, for He is the Creator. Yet, He was born in the likeness of men. Jesus was recognized as Joseph's (the carpenter) son. No sane person would argue that Jesus the Nazarene didn't walk this earth. Isaiah tells us that once Messiah (Jesus) was crucified, His form was beyond mankind. He was unrecognizable.

Perhaps, some people keep their distance from you when you're suffering, not because they've changed (no longer being your friend), but because you've been changed by suffering.

Job's suffering, though far less than Jesus' suffering, reveals a similar fate. In Job 2:11-12, the Bible says:

Now when Job's three friends heard of all this evil that had come upon him...they made an appointment together to come to show him sympathy and comfort him. And when they saw him from a distance, they did not recognize him.

Suffering left both Jesus and Job unrecognizable. Some of the people you think are the closest to you keep their distance from you when you're suffering. You've probably heard it said from a person in the midst of suffering:

"You learn who your real friends are when you suffer."

Yes, there is some truth to that statement, but it may be unfair to use that as a blanket statement. Perhaps, some people keep their distance from you when you're suffering, not because they've changed (no longer being your friend), but because you've been changed by suffering. Maybe they don't recognize you and because of that they don't feel like they can help you. Don't be too hard on the friends and family who are absent amidst your suffering. Also, don't be too hard on the family and friends who are present during your suffering. Job's friends started out great, but turned out to be a disaster.

His words cut deep. A pastor friend of mine and his wife are separated. The separation crushed him. I asked him what God was teaching him. At his lowest point, God used another pastor to speak a word to him about people being absent during his time of suffering. God delivered him from the lies of Satan. Satan was telling him that he should take his own life because no one cared. But God. God told him that others were absent because suffering caused him to be unrecognizable. God began to put *already and not yet* people into his life. That is, people he already knew and people he didn't know yet. God is aware and God cares.

Why do bad things happen to good people?

Why do bad things happen to good people? Oh, how this question is flawed. Why yes, it may be an honest question from the one asking, but it is flawed. The answer is hard to swallow because this has only happened once. Only one time in human history has anything bad happened to a good person—Jesus. On this side of the cross, the truth is, bad things don't happen to good people. For there are no good people, save Jesus. But the result of these bad things (Jesus' suffering) happening to Jesus is that Jesus saves.

Job didn't charge God with wrong, but he also didn't charge himself with wrong. Job was right by not charging God with wrong. Job was wrong by also not charging himself with wrong. Maybe you have charged God with wrong. I know I have, but God has shown me that I was wrong in charging God with wrong. Jesus is right. All of us are wrong; however, Jesus is making all wrongs right!

She Says

Sam and I refer to everything as BC and AC. Before cancer and after cancer. We will never see or experience life the same again. Cancer is now four years in our rearview mirror and still there's not a day that goes by that I don't think of it at least 100 times.

At the end of Job Chapter 2, when Job's friends show up, verses 12 & 13 tell us,

> *And they raised their voices and wept, and they tore their robes and sprinkled dust on their heads toward heaven. And they sat with him on the ground seven days and seven nights, and no one spoke a word to him, for they saw that his suffering was very great.*

His friends were humbly mourning with him. Job's anguish was so deep that no one said a word for seven days and nights. This had to stir their souls because if this could happen to a good ole boy like Job, it could happen to them too.

A summary of the beginning of Job Chapter 1 tells us Job was an "upright" man," "feared God and turned away from evil," "consecrated his children" and "rose early in the morning to make burnt offerings." Job was also immensely blessed in earthly treasures as well as had a family we'd all die for. Lots of children who threw him banquets (I love a good pool party with my kids), a large number of servants and livestock, and verse 3 says,

> ...this man was the greatest of all the people of the east.

Job was blessed and highly favored!

Like many believers, I like to think bad things don't happen to "good" people. Like Sam said, we'd checked off the box of doing all the "good" things. Geez, we'd sold everything we had to move to the middle of nowhere to serve Him. And we stayed there, never sending out resumes, never seeking to leave. We are no Jobs, but we tried to look out for others, tithed, volunteered everywhere under the sun, went on all the mission trips, made sure our girls were always in church, exercised daily, and ate healthy enough (except for Mayfield cookies and cream ice cream every now and then—who can resist that!). Cancer was not supposed to happen to us. That was not what Sam and I were thinking when we said, "in sickness and in health." That was only for "other" people.

Cancer did change us though. For the better. Hard things can do that. They can make us better, or they can make us bitter. We had all the feels. Peace, anger, joy, resentment, gratitude, sadness. Sometimes we'd feel all those things on the same day, in the same hour.

After the diagnosis, word got around pretty quickly. We'd briefly considered keeping it quiet, but that would never work. For one thing, I'm such an open book. I can't lie to save my life. And that would have taken a lot of lying by omission. Second, we wanted the prayers. We were in way over our heads. Sam even posted regular videos to share on social media to keep up with answering questions. I seriously don't know what people without Jesus and a church family do in times like these. We had an outpouring of love and support that we'll never be able to repay. Find you a good Bible believing church and find your tribe! You need an army of like-minded believers for these hard things that will come your way!

We also heard some things we wished we could have unheard. I love how Job's friends showed up, and for seven days and nights they just sat with him in silence. They didn't know what to say so they sat in silence. But their silence was the wisest thing they could have done.

Suffering in silence is hard, we want to fix things, we want to say the perfect thing to make it all make sense. They should have stayed in silence because if they'd had a pair of Jessica Simpson's on, they definitely stuck them in their mouths shortly after they opened them. Because, for the next several chapters, they try to make sense of it by telling Job how it was his fault and he must have done something terribly wrong to deserve all the pain and loss.

For days I refused to cry. I knew that once it happened, I wouldn't be able to turn it off. So, I kept that stiff upper lip, we consoled our friends and family, and Sam and I insisted it would be ok. This was before we knew that it would be ok. This was when it was stage four, very advanced, had spread, and many of my organs were compromised. It had been there for years. A friend sent me a well-meaning message telling me about a friend she knew who had been battling cancer for several years and that I could do it too. And that did it, my heart broke for this momma. The flood works came, and they didn't stop for days. I couldn't fight cancer for years. I just couldn't. And the thought of leaving my poor girls to be raised without their mom haunted my every thought. I laid in the floor like a 2-year-old throwing a tantrum and screamed at God. I remember one night getting out of bed in the middle of the night sobbing, not wanting to wake Sam. So, I went and laid in the floor of my closet and cried. I didn't want him to know.

In Job Chapters 20-22, Job's "friends" continue to cast blame on him likely because it made them feel better. If this could happen to Job, it could happen to anyone, and we don't like to think about misery happening to us when we don't "deserve" it. Psalms 139:6 says,

GOSPEL CONVERSATIONAL MARRIAGE

Such knowledge is too wonderful for me; it is high; I cannot attain it.

We can't know God's reasons for what He does. How often have we too blamed ourselves or others for bad things that happen. God has His own reasons for letting us suffer.

Harold and Maida Sedman are the epitome of the "in sickness" end-of-the-stick right now. In 61 years of marriage, Harold has always been the servant leader, looking after orphans and widows and serving the church faithfully. And he's always driven our church groups wherever we needed to go. He loves to drive. If his schedule was free, he was there bright and early with the bus clean and full of gas. There's no one I'd trust more than Mr. Harold to drive our busload through the winding mountain roads of Boone, North Carolina. to serve at the processing center for Operation Christmas Child. Sure, there are closer and more convenient processing centers, but the Boone headquarters feels to me like Disney World does to everyone else. And he was always game.

I hadn't seen them in a while, so I sent her a message to check in. Turns out Mr. Harold has dementia coming on and some eye troubles that have robbed him of his ability to drive. Mrs. Maida now does the driving and the care taking despite her own health struggles. Even through these great challenges, Mrs. Maida is as gracious as ever. I'm sure, like the rest of us, the "in sickness" part wasn't what she was focusing on when she said her vows 61 years ago.

Bad things do happen to "good" people. If nothing bad has ever happened to you, either you are just "the glass is half full" kind of person or it will. It's just good for character building. And who wants the character of someone who gets their way all the time. Going through cancer made Sam and me lean into and onto God like never before. I wouldn't change a thing. We can minister better to those suffering around us now that we have experienced it ourselves.

WHEN you face "in sickness," lean into God, not away from Him. Learn whatever it is that He's trying to show you. God is always working. Find Him, and go there. You can be mad at him for a minute if you need to, but don't stay there.

Being part of an amazing church family during that time was priceless. The hardest thing for us to overcome was letting others help. Let others help you during your suffering and sickness. I really wanted to protect our girls from the fear of the unknown at that time. I planned everything out so they wouldn't feel the horror of the situation. I guess I did a really good job because they both remember loving all of the friends that helped out with car rides and ball games, food that flooded our house and visits from our community that huddled in tight and guarded us from the enemy. I miss that part.

In Job 42:7, God rebukes Job's friends for misrepresenting Him. It wasn't anything Job had done to cause all of the bad things that had happened. God is God, He will do as He pleases, and Job knew and accepted that. We have to accept that too.

Then. Y'all. Job prays for his friends. The ones who accused him and threw stones at him during the deepest devastation imaginable. Could you do that?

In verse 10 of Chapter 42, Scripture tells us that the Lord restored his fortune and family. He not only restored it, but He doubled the blessing that Job had before. I know it's hard for us parents to understand how you can replace kids, but we have to know that God is faithful and just. And we know, as believers, Job would meet them again on the other side of Heaven. Then it gets even better. Job lived another 140 years and got to enjoy his children's children's children's children.

Sam and I were definitely changed by our "in sickness" season. Thankfully it was just that—a season. None of us know what our future holds, but He does. I'd definitely say our suffering made us better. Lean into your marriage, honor your vows, stay faithful to His will. God will bless you and your marriage through the suffering.

xoxo

CONVERSATION STARTERS

1. Read Job 1. Discuss with your spouse how Satan works to destroy your marriage and family.

2. Read Job 2. Discuss what you and your spouse can learn and apply from Job and his wife's dialogue.

3. In what ways are you being too hard on yourself as a caregiver in your marriage? In what ways are you being too hard on yourself as a patient in your marriage?

4. Discuss how suffering has changed your marriage. Discuss how suffering could change your marriage.

SAM & TONYA GREER

Conversation 9

Sex is a Good Thang

Let my beloved come to his garden, and eat its choicest fruits. I came to my garden, my sister, my bride, I gathered my myrrh with my spice, I ate my honeycomb with my honey, I drank my wine with my milk.
Song of Solomon 4:16, 5:1

Whose idea was sex anyway? Why is sex outside of marriage unhealthy and harmful? How is sex in marriage more about giving than getting? What do you do when you and your spouse have different sex drives?

The Song That Wil Get Your Husband to Church

Songs are not at the top of my what-gets-men-to-church list. Music may or may not be what draws men to church, but what if I told you there is a particular Song that will reach churched, unchurched, dechurched, rechurched, echurched, and never-been-to-church husbands alike? Would any of you wives be interested? Wives, I bet you are standing at the ready to add that Song to your husband's Spotify or Amazon Music playlist. Rather than simply syncing this Song to your husband's phone, start singing this Song in your homes. Douglas O'Donnell gives us a scenario of this Song being sung in the home:

> Think with me for a moment. Imagine a woman coming to church for the first time in ten years. She hears a sermon [based on the unabashed celebration of marital sex found in the Song of Songs]. When she returns home after the service, her husband is reclining on the couch, watching the football game. It's a commercial, so he generously mutes the television and asks,
>
> "So how was it?"
>
> "Fine," she says.
>
> "Well, what did the pastor talk about?"
>
> "Oh," she says, "he talked about how wives should be more aggressive in bed."
>
> "What!" He turns off the TV.
>
> "Yeah, he said something about how wives should be more aggressive in bed. It's in the Bible, I guess. Some book called the Song of Songs."
>
> "Really?"
>
> "Yeah, really."
>
> He looks down, rubs his chin, and murmurs,
>
> "So, what time is the service next week?" [lii]

The Song of Solomon is a song that husbands would not only listen to, but also sing and maybe even rap!

Sex Is a God Thang

Sex without marriage is not good. Marriage without sex is not good. Sex in marriage is very good. How can we know that sex in marriage is very good? Genesis 1:27, 31; 2:18 and 24 give us at least two reasons that sex in marriage is good:

So God created man in his own image, in the image of God he created him; male and female he created them…And God saw everything that he had made, and behold, it was very good…Then the LORD God said, "It is not good that the man should be alone; I will make him a helper fit for him."…Therefore a man shall leave his father and mother and hold fast to his wife, and they shall become one flesh.

First, after each day of creation, God looked at His creation and said *it was good,* until the last day. On the last day of creation God made Adam and Eve and said *it was very good.* Did you hear the difference? Very good is always better than good. God only said His creation was *very good* after He made the two (Adam and Eve) to become one. Sex within marriage is one of the prominent ways the two become one. Are you with me? Sex in marriage, then, is very good. Second, prior to the creation of Eve, Adam looked lost and God said *it is not good that man should be alone.* God made Eve *from* Adam and *for* Adam. Adam and Eve became one flesh and it was so very good that they were both naked and unashamed. That's what I call very good! Tim Keller, in his book *The Meaning of Marriage,* wrote:

> Indeed, sex is perhaps the most powerful God-created way to help you give your entire self to another human being. Sex is

God's appointed way for two people to reciprocally say to one another, "I belong completely, permanently, and exclusively to you." You must not use sex to say anything less. So, according to the Bible, a covenant (marriage) is necessary for sex. It creates a place of security for vulnerability and intimacy. But though a marriage covenant is necessary for sex, sex is also necessary for the maintenance of the covenant (marriage).[liii]

Biblical marriage is needed for sex, but sex is also needed for biblical marriage.

Sex was created for a lifetime, not a lifestyle. Sex was created for a till-death-do-us-part lifetime, not a till-dawn-do-us-part lifestyle.

Biblical marriage is necessary for sex. Let's flesh this out further. No pun intended. Yeah, right. The sexual revolution in our world today is a revolt against God's Word. Sex outside of marriage is out-of-control in our culture. Yet, sex outside of marriage is out-of-bounds according to the Bible. Why? Is God a cosmic killjoy who only desires to kill your joy? No. God knows that sex outside of the bonds of marriage, between one man and one woman, is harmful and unhealthy. Having sex outside of marriage may increase the likelihood of abuse as a sexual connection may cause the abused to stay in that abusive relationship. Sex outside of biblical marriage is unhealthy as there is no commitment, no trust, no legal, cultural, moral, familial, or societal obligation from either party. From a biblical worldview, sex is reserved for the marriage relationship between one husband and one wife.

In Song of Solomon 4:16-5:1 Solomon and the Shulamite woman were talking about sex in marriage:

Let my beloved come to his garden, and eat its choicest fruits. I came to my garden, my sister, my bride, I gathered my myrrh with my spice, I ate my honeycomb with my honey, I drank my wine with my milk.

The churched are as confused about sex inside of marriage as the unchurched are confused about sex outside of marriage.

Some of y'all thinking…uh…THAT'S in the Bible? Yep, it's in there! In fact, this section of Scripture, which is the consummation of Solomon and the Shulamite woman's marriage, is also the climax of the book. This text, which falls in the center of the book, confirms that God designed sex within the confines of biblical marriage. C. S. Lewis correlated sex outside of marriage with tasting and chewing food without swallowing and then spitting it out.[liv] How interesting that marriage, where God gave the gift of sex, is a lifetime covenant. Sex was created for a lifetime, not a lifestyle. Sex was created for a till-death-do-us-part lifetime, not a till-dawn-do-us-part lifestyle. Any and all sex outside of biblical marriage is sin. Biblical marriage is necessary for sex.

Sex is necessary for biblical marriage. The churched are as confused about sex inside of marriage as the unchurched are confused about sex outside of marriage. Churched folk think of sex as taboo, until we get married. Then, in marriage, sex is merely tolerated, but not celebrated. In marriage, sex is treated like the little brother who is a bother. No! Celebrate sex in marriage! Wake up, church! Sex is not simply permitted in marriage, but it's prescribed for marriage. Sex is not simply a marriage nicety, but it's a marriage necessity. Read that again! Don't get me wrong—nookie in marriage is nice (or should I say *NOICE*), but it's also necessary. You see, God gave us sex in marriage for at least three reasons.

1. Protection. God has called us to remain pure and flee from sexual immorality. He didn't give this command and then say *good luck* with that. God gave us the gift of marriage for protection against sexual immorality. God always gives us a way of escape from temptation and sex in marriage is one of those ways. Paul, in 1 Corinthians 7:2-5, wrote:

> But because of the temptation to sexual immorality, each man should have his own wife and each woman her own husband. The husband should give to his wife her conjugal rights, and likewise the wife to her husband. For the wife does not have authority over her own body, but the husband does. Likewise the husband does not have authority over his body, but the wife does. Do not deprive one another, except perhaps by agreement for a limited time, that you may devote yourselves to prayer; but then come together again, so that Satan may not tempt you because of your lack of self-control.

Sex in marriage helps protect against the ongoing onslaught of the temptation of sexual immorality. Paul's words fly in the face of the ancient world's hypocrisy that wives were the possession of their husbands, but husbands were not the possession of their wives. The fact that both husband and wife do not have *authority over* their own bodies slammed the door on husbands being allowed to have multiple sexual partners. Both husband and wife solely and exclusively belong to the other.

Marriage is the perfect place for imperfect people to be protected from sexual immorality.

The COVID-19 pandemic of 2020 caused 62.5% of engaged couples to postpone their weddings. In 2019, the wedding market reported 2.13 million weddings. The number of weddings in 2020 plunged to 1.1 million (47% decrease), while 2.77 million (30% increase) weddings are forecasted for 2021.[iv] Why share this information with you? COVID-19 may have postponed weddings, but do you think this virus postponed the temptation of sexual immorality. Did COVID-19 somehow remove engaged couples from tempting and compromising situations that lead to sexual acts which are reserved for marriage? I know engaged couples postponed getting married because they wanted the perfect wedding, but God is more interested in your marriage than your wedding. Couples, if you know you are going to end up together, then get married sooner, not later. Marriage is the perfect place for imperfect people to be protected from sexual immorality.

2. Procreation. BREAKING NEWS: Men can't bear or birth children. I know the world says men can bear and birth children, but the Word says, in Genesis 3:16:

*To the **woman** he said, "I will surely multiply your pain in childbearing."*

I highlighted *woman* for a reason. Women, not men, were created with the ability and responsibility to bear and birth children. Marriage, then, is the context by which God commands men and women to procreate. The first thing God said...*man, I love this*...the first thing God said to Adam and Eve...*say it loud for the people in the back*...the first thing God said to Adam and Eve after creating them... *this is oh so good*...is found in Genesis 1:28:

And God blessed them. And God said to them, "Be fruitful and multiply and fill the earth and subdue it..."

And every husband of every tribe, language, nation, and people said...Hallelujah! Hallelujah! Hallelujah! Hallelujah! You don't think sex is a God thang? The very first thing God said to Adam and Eve was *be fruitful and multiply.*

God's desire is to populate the earth, not depopulate the earth.

Did you know that Israel (God's people) increased greatly while in slavery in Egypt? Joseph died at the end of Genesis, but a new day begins in Exodus 1:6-7:

Then Joseph died, and all his brothers and all that generation. But the people of Israel were fruitful and increased greatly; they multiplied and grew exceedingly strong, so that the land was filled with them.

Isn't it a marvelous thought that God used procreation to populate and strengthen His own people while they were in slavery in Egypt? Whether one is living in the times of anti-Yahweh Egypt or living in the times of anti-Bible, anti-God, anti-gospel, and anti-Christ America, God created marriage for procreation. God's desire is to populate the earth, not depopulate the earth. God uses procreation to populate the earth in order that heaven will be populated by those who place their faith alone by grace alone in Jesus alone.

God is pleased when husband and wife sexually pleasure one another.

3. Pleasure. Sex in marriage is not only for procreation, but it is also for recreation. That's right! Procreate and recreate. Married couples, get your reps in! God delights in husbands and wives delighting in one another. God is pleased when husband and wife sexually pleasure one another. How can we know that God desires for married couples to delight in one another sexually? The Holy Spirit reminds us that sexual intimacy is for our delight in Proverbs 5:18-19:

Let your fountain be blessed, and rejoice in the wife of your youth, a lovely deer, a graceful doe. Let her breasts fill you at all times with delight; be intoxicated always in her love.

Tonya thinks that I always think about sex. I tell her that it's her fault. I am *intoxicated always in her love*. In his book *Marriage and the Mystery of the Gospel*, Ray Ortlund describes sex in marriage like a fire in the fireplace:

> The key to understanding the sexual wisdom of [the Bible] is to combine both form and freedom, both structure and liberation. Conservative people love form and restraint and control. Progressive people love freedom and openness and choices. Both see part of the truth, but wisdom sees more. Wisdom teaches us that God gave us our sexuality both to focus our romantic joy and to unleash our romantic joy. When our desires are both focused and unleashed—both form and freedom—our sexual experience becomes wonderfully intensified. A marriage can flourish within both form and freedom, because sex is like a fire. In the fireplace, it keeps us warm. Outside the fireplace, it burns the house down. Here's the message of the Bible: 'Keep the fire within the marital fireplace, and stoke that fire as hot as you can.'[lvi]

Puritan Richard Baxter once said to a husband and wife:

"Keep up your conjugal love in a constant heat and vigor."[lvii]

Amen! Husbands and wives, make your sex life as hot as you can and enjoy it. Married couples, God enjoys you enjoying one another sexually.

Sex Is a Good Thang

A pastor friend of mine and his wife pray before having sex thanking God for the *good gift they are about to receive*. All good gifts come from our Father above, but it will be hard from now on for you to keep a straight face when someone prays, *thank you Lord for this good gift we are about to receive*, at the table before a meal. The Bible portrays sex in marriage as a good thang. It's not a bad thing, not a dirty thing, not a shameful thing, not an embarrassing thing, but a good thang. Sex in marriage is not a shamefully bad thing; on the contrary it's a shockingly good thang.

We can't say it, write it, hear it, believe it, know it, and live it enough that sex in marriage is about body sharing, not body shaming.

Marital body sharing > body shaming. Body shaming is the practice of subjecting someone to criticism or mockery for supposed bodily faults or imperfections.[lviii] In a world where body shaming has become the norm, the Bible paints the most non-body-shaming picture in history. The Bible is pro-body. Tonya has me taking some probiotic stuff for gut health. I don't know if the Bible is pro-probiotic, but I am thankful that the Bible is pro-body. I know I am pro-Tonya's-body! Amen! Speaking about God's view of the human body, Tim Keller wrote:

> Biblical Christianity may be the most body-positive religion in the world. It teaches that God made matter and physical bodies and saw that is was all good (Genesis 1:31). It says that in Jesus Christ God himself actually took on a human body (which he still has in glorified form), and that someday he is going to give us all perfect, resurrected bodies. It says that God created sexuality and gave a woman and man to each other in the beginning.[lix]

Thank God Almighty that sex in marriage is not about body shaming, but body sharing. A husband is not to body shame his wife, but share his body with his wife. A wife is not to body shame her husband, but share her body with her husband. We can't say it, write it, hear it, believe it, know it, and live it enough that sex in marriage is about body sharing, not body shaming. Take for example The Song of Solomon 4:1-2 and 7:1-9:

Your hair is like a flock of goats leaping down the slopes of Gilead. Your teeth are like a flock of shorn ewes that have come up from the washing, all of which bear twins, and not one among them has lost its young…Your rounded thighs are like jewels, the work of a master hand. Your navel is a rounded bowl that never lacks mixed wine. Your belly is a heap of wheat, encircled with lilies. Your two breasts are like two fawns, twins of a gazelle. Your neck is like an ivory tower. Your eyes are pools in Heshbon, by the gate of Bath-rabbim. Your nose is like a tower of Lebanon, which looks toward Damascus. Your head crowns you like Carmel, and your flowing locks are like purple; a king is held captive in the tresses. How beautiful and pleasant are you, O loved one, with all your delights! Your stature is like a palm tree, and your breasts are like its clusters. I say I will climb the palm tree and lay hold of its fruit. O may your breasts be like clusters of the vine, and the scent of your breath like apples, and your mouth like the best wine.

Yep, it's about time for you and your spouse to do a Bible study in The Song of Solomon. Though some of this language seems strange, Solomon is not body shaming his beloved. He is praising her beauty as they prepare to share their bodies. Body sharing > body shaming in marriage, and that's a good thang.

    Marital body sharing is intimate, generous, and builds trust through transparency. What better way to build trust than to be open and transparent. What better way to be open and transparent than to uncover the most private parts of you and your spouse's body and offer them to one another in marriage. Spouses see one another's scars and all in the nakedness of marriage. Sex in marriage helps build trust as it encourages transparency not just physically but emotionally, spiritually, psychologically, and relationally.

Sharing one another's bodies with one another generates generosity in the marriage relationship between spouses. Generating generosity sexually will also open the door for you and your spouse to be generous emotionally, relationally, spiritually, and psychologically. Understand, husband and wife, you are the only one who can biblically meet the sexual needs of your spouse. So. Be. Generous. *It's better to give than to get* is one of my favorite biblical principles. Marriage is about giving not getting. Keller, again, speaks of the importance of giving one another sexual pleasure in marriage:

> Each partner in marriage is to be most concerned not with getting sexual pleasure but with giving it. In short, the greatest pleasure should be the pleasure of seeing your spouse getting pleasure. When you get to the place where giving arousal is the most arousing thing, you are practicing this principle.[ix]

Husbands, focus on the sexual interest of your wife. Wives, focus on the sexual interest of your husband. How do we focus on one another's sexual interests if we don't know one another's sexual interests?

Talk about sex more, not less. I wish someone had talked to Tonya and me fifteen years ago about talking about sex more, not less. It took us a while to figure this out, but we are working on it more each day (get those reps in). In particular, there was something in our sex life that we had failed to communicate about. Now that we have, it's even more fun than before. Tell your spouse what you like. Ask your spouse what he or she likes. I know this can seem uncomfortable, but nothing is more comforting in marriage than being totally vulnerable.

She loves lamp. He hates lamp.

Tonya loves lamps, but I loathe lamps. She loves lamp. He hates lamp. Tonya loves to have lamps on all the time. Well, almost all the time. The only time when I want the lamp to be turned on is the only time Tonya insists the lamp be turned off. You got it, nookie time. Then, when we are finished with nookie, she turns the lamp right back on. Ugh! Let me be fair, there are times when Tonya lets the lamp stay on. Talk about what you like and what you don't like. Talk about sex more, not less.

Have sex more, not less. Having more conversations about sex is great, but having more sex is greater. Married couples need to have more sex, not less. While teaching a marriage series, Ed Young Jr. challenged husbands and wives to have sex once a day for seven days (seven days of sex). Ed Young Jr.'s dad, Ed Sr., responded to his son's challenge with these words:

"Once a day!? Your mom and I will try to dial it back to only once a day."[lxi]

Ed Jr. pointed out that since married couples have said "I do" then they should *do it!*[lxii] What do you do when your spouse doesn't want to *do it?*

Tonya wrote a poem which includes a reminder that spouses often have different sex drives in marriage.

My Baggy Red Sweats

My baggy red sweats, are old and worn.
They have tiny holes, where they have been torn.

They are faded and stretched, and short at the bottom.
But they are comfy and cozy, so that is no problem.

They've been thru two babies, so they rarely fit right.
Sometimes they are baggy, sometimes they are tight.

They were passed from my mother, so worth every penny,

SAM & TONYA GREER

But when the hubs sees me in them, he knows, he ain't gettin any.

He has tried to convince me to get rid of the things
But I can't bring myself to replace them with jeans.

For they are my comfort when my hectic day ends
And all is quiet, but the clean-up begins.

I've searched high and low to find a more flattering pair,
But when it comes to versatility, no others compare.

So to my baggy red sweats for now I'll hold onto
Because when it comes to throwing them out, I simply don't want to.

And for all of my friends who have been so lucky to find
Those baggy red sweats, that are one of a kind.

May your journey together, like ours be long
And your hard days go by fast, so your sweats you can put on![lxiii]

In marriage, what do you do when you don't want to *do it*? I know that husbands almost always want to do it. Who am I kidding? We husbands always want to do it. How do you put sex in overdrive when both spouses have different sex drives? A wife may only want to have sex once a week, but a husband wants sex every day. What do you do? The line in Tonya's poem that reads, *But when the hubs sees me in them, he knows, he ain't gettin any*, reiterates the fact that I am ready for sex anytime even when I ain't getting any.

Oh, the never-ending tension one spouse wanting sex while the other doesn't—*IS* the elephant that never leaves the room. What should a wife do who is not in the mood but whose husband is? She should be willing to serve her husband sexually because Christ has served her. What should a husband do who is in the mood, but whose wife isn't? He should be willing to patiently wait because Christ has been so patient with him.[lxiv] Let sex in your marriage be about out-serving one another, not holding out on one another.

Let Me Holla at the Husbands

Pornography is lying to you. Satan is lying to you. There is no greater sex in the world than sex between a husband and a wife in a committed marriage relationship. It's not even close. Some treat sex as a god. Sex should never be viewed as a god, but sex is a God thang. It was created by God. It was God's idea. Sex is not only a God thang and a good thang, but sex is also a gospel thang. Husbands, there is a word in Scripture used to describe the sexual intimacy between husband and wife: *know*. The Bible refers to sex as a matter of *knowing* a spouse. When Cain was born, the Bible says in Genesis 4:1:

Now Adam knew Eve his wife, and she conceived and bore Cain.

Know in the original language means "sexual relations," "have sexual intercourse," "know through personal experience," "arrive at the knowledge of someone," or "come to know."[lxv] I am trying to get to KNOW Tonya best I can all day, erry day! Guys, we must spend time getting to know our wives. What does she like? What turns her on? What turns her off? What gets her going? What issues does she care about? What is she scared of? What makes her feel safe? What makes her feel loved? What makes her feel wanted? What makes her feel sexy? Are you speaking her language? If you want to get some loving, then you better learn her love language and speak it!

Intimacy in our relationship as husband and wife is an overflow of our intimacy with the Lord Jesus. Intimacy is God's idea. The Bible emphasizes the union between God the Father, God the Son, and God the Holy Spirit. Jesus prayed about His union with the Father in John 17. All three persons of the Godhead magnify and glorify one another.

God desires for you to know Him, not just know about Him. Husbands, get in the Word. Stay in the Word. Be the church. Be at church. You must lead your family to Jesus and keep them in church. Speaking about the importance of church, Tony Evans said:

> I hear people say, 'I don't have to go to church to be a Christian,' and they are absolutely right. Salvation is through faith alone in Christ alone. But you don't have to go home to be married, but stay away long enough and your relationship will be affected.[lxvi]

As you grow closer to Jesus and His church, then you will be able to grow closer to your wife. Husbands, it's on us to lead our family to Jesus and His church.

Do you know your spouse? It was so embarrassing. Tonya and I were part of a newlywed game in our first church. We didn't do too well. We lost. I said her eyes were brown, but they are green. I would chalk it up as being color blind, but I'm not color blind. I felt like the husband at the counseling retreat who, when the speaker said that couples are so disconnected that 85% of husbands don't know their wife's favorite flower, looked at his wife and said:

"Your favorite flower is self-rising, isn't it?"

Husband, pay attention to your wife. Spend time with her. Focus on her. See her. Pursue her. Serve her. Comfort her. Learn her. Listen to her. Delight in her. Tell her you delight in her. Ask her good quality questions. Get started by asking her some of these questions:

- How can I pray for you?

- What do you need from me?

- How can I provide comfort, safety and security when you feel anxious or nervous?

- How can we improve the quality of our time together?

- How can I help you accomplish your goals?

- What goals would you like to set as a couple?

- Are there people you would like for us to spend time getting to know?

- What can I do better to serve you?

- Is there something you would like for us to do together?

- What can we do to be better connected?

To set the mood in the bedroom, make room for engaging her in conversation.

She Says

Mercy. This is not the chapter I have been looking forward to. Sam, however, Could…Not…Wait. Insert eye roll here. I've been a little stressed over book writing the last few days so tonight, Sam sent me to his office. I know it's going to confuse some folks around here to see my car parked in his spot on the corner of 4000 Dayton Blvd in Chattanooga, but I needed some time out of the house. Too many distractions.

Sam hates when I'm out of the house. I barely do those girls' night out kinda things because my man is just not a fan. I think it's mostly because he knows "he ain't getting any," but he'll never admit it. So, I was stunned when he offered to send me out of the house. I quickly packed my bag and squealed out of the driveway.

And that man has one thing on his mind when he gets home. I like to hear about his day, but all he wants to do is grope me and ask if and when he's getting some. He harasses me until I say something resembling a yes. But, as usual, I have other things on my mind. Kids have to be fed, the kitchen has to be cleaned, the dog needs to go out, etc., etc., etc.

I like our girls. I love being with our girls, shopping with our girls, getting my hair done with our girls, working out with our girls, sitting and just doing nothing with our girls. I love to know everything going on with them. My parents were divorced when I was very young, and I didn't get to see my mom as much as most kids do. So, I guess I'm also making sure they never feel that void. But they are amazing kids, and I just enjoy them. As wives, we are constantly juggling so many things. I thrive on juggling tons and tons of "stuff." It can become very easy to put my man on the back burner. Guilty. And sometimes I'm just plain exhausted. Here's a little secret between you and me—*sometimes I stay "busy" until he goes to sleep.* Yes, I do! He goes to work out really early in the mornings so he can't handle much past 10 p.m. He's out cold! I do a silent *"YES!"* to myself when I've scored a night off! Tell me I'm not the only one.

Then I feel a twinge of guilt. Poor fella. He asks so little of me. That's pretty much all he asks of me. He doesn't care if I cook or clean or water the plants. He doesn't care that I'm not the picture-perfect pastor's wife. He lets me get my hair done and pretty much get whatever I want. I kinda have it made. He just likes that one thing that I'm always tryna worm my way out of. Bless.

Ladies, when we "deprive" our fellas, we put them at greater risk. The temptation for men to look at porn is nearly irresistible. Most men, in fact, can't resist it. And did you know when one or both partners are looking at porn regularly, they are doubling their already high chances for divorce. And most men and women don't stop watching porn once they start. The sin ensnares them and, without help, it's really hard to stop. We all have these little convenience devices in our back pocket that make it so hard to say "no." There's little to no accountability with them, and most families have put one in the hands of their kids by the time they are 12 years old. No wonder our world is so messed up. In America we have all the "freedoms" that really do nothing but bind us up and enslave us to Satan.

After all the surgeries from cancer, my stomach looked like a road map of scars. Still does. Initially I was paranoid and self-conscious about them. I didn't want Sam to see them and I was constantly covering myself. I have what's called a zipper—a scar that runs from the bottom of the rib cage to the top of the pelvic bone. And I have all kinds of other scars from tubes coming in and out during surgery. Somewhere along the way I became proud of the thing that once gave me such shame. Going through that was HARD. But Sam and I went through that together. He earned that scar as much as I did, and now I happily show it off like a warrior badge.

Your "scars" may be something else. Whatever is holding you back, causing you shame, and stealing your joy in the bedroom, release it. Let it go. You and your fella have earned every battle wound together. That extra tire you carry around, those stretch marks, that c-section scar from birthing his children, his legacy. Don't let that shame you into not enjoying your man. Wear them proudly. Be faithful to your man.

In the Greer house, we like peanut butter. Peanut butter rice cakes, peanut butter and blueberry sandwiches, peanut butter crackers, Reese's peanut butter cereal, peanut butter balls. We also keep an open jar of peanut butter just for scooping with a spoon. We ALWAYS have lots and lots of kids in our house and they know the pantry and all the snacks are there for the taking. No need to ask, just get what you want. But stay out of the peanut butter! We are double dippers!

We may double dip our peanut butter, but don't double dip in your marriage. Many things contribute to the infidelity epidemic in

America such as boredom, porn, addictions, "growing apart," lack of respect, feeling unappreciated, the internet. We can come up with all kinds of excuses, but Scripture tells us in Hebrews 13:4:

> Let marriage be held in honor among all, and let the marriage bed be undefiled, for God will judge the sexually immoral and adulterous.

Sexual immorality is any kind of sexual activity outside of marriage between a man and a woman. One of the cool things about working in Sam's office is being able to grab a commentary off the shelves. Mercy this man has a lot of commentaries. Do you know what his second favorite thing to do is? Write sermons. In John MacArthur's New Testament commentary on Hebrews, he talks of a publisher of a leading pornographic magazine who maintains that,

> Sex is a function of the body, a drive which man shares with animals, like eating, drinking and sleeping. It's a physical demand that must be satisfied. If you don't satisfy it, you will have all sorts of neurosis and repressive psychoses. Sex is here to stay; let's forget the prudery that makes us hide from it. Throw away those inhibitions, find a girl who's like-minded and let yourself go.[lxvii]

Oh, my soul, I'm so glad I'm not married to him! Honor your marriage bed, cut out the porn, get in the Word, and get some accountability. Sam and the rest of the men on staff have an app for accountability. It's a web browser called Accountable2You. This means you have to delete other web browsers from your device and not cheat by using them. There is a fee for this app, but anytime you step out of line with your searches, whoever you select as your accountability partner will get notified. Sam has it set up where I get a notification about his web searches. At 3 a.m. Every. Single. Day. And every single day, Accountable2You tells me he's made 0 inappropriate web searches. If you or your fella struggle with this—yes women struggle with it too—this is a small price to pay to get some accountability for yourself. The temptations are real. Satan is real. And he's here to destroy your marriage. It's getting dark in Sam's office. He has no lamps. I have failed him. Tomorrow I shop for lamps. Shopping and lamps. My two fav things.

And it's nearing 10pm. I just might get myself off the hook tonight. ;)

xoxo

CONVERSATION STARTERS

1. Read Song of Solomon together and discuss. How does God view sex in marriage? How should you?

2. Ask your spouse what they want before having sex. Talk about sex more with your spouse. Tell him or her what you like.

3. Husbands and wives, what do you struggle with the most in your sex life? Do you use sex in ways that serve your spouse or serve yourself? Do you withhold sex as a means of getting your way or punishing your spouse?

4. In what ways can you flirt with your spouse? What is some intimate foreplay that both of you will enjoy?

Conversation 10

Social Media and Scriptural Marriage

Though I have much to write to you, I would rather not use paper or ink. Instead I hope to come to you and talk face to face, so that our joy may be complete.
2 John 12

What guardrails should be in place in your marriage to fight against adultery? What about singleness? How is social media affecting marriage and family? How should husbands and wives limit social media usage?

The Other Woman

It was all on me. My fault. Totally. Tonya and I had only been married a few years and living away from home in Bush, Louisiana. We had a date night scheduled. I was to meet her for dinner when she got off work that Friday evening. I stood her up. Terrible, I know. The other woman had me occupied as she was in need. She was hurting. She was falling apart. She needed help. She had just experienced a devastating storm and I was going to be her hero. I was going to be her savior. The other woman was the local church. I had been working all day that Friday helping local churches with hurricane Katrina relief. You want to talk about relief. Good grief! Hurricane Katrina had Bush, Louisiana looking like a war zone. Tornadoes whittled down trees into toothpicks and piled them on the roadways like it was a lumber yard. For miles, Highway LA 41 disappeared under tornado debris. Some folks in Bush were without power for two months after Katrina. Paying attention to the other woman all that day only resulted in me standing up my wife for date night.

Tonya wasn't happy. She was the opposite of happy. Tonya was just about to leave Bush and head back home to her mom. I messed up. You see, this wasn't the first time as a young pastor that I put the other woman, the church, before Tonya. I apologized. I begged her to stay. She was gracious and stayed. I wrote a rap song sometime later which captures this part of our testimony in verse two. So, stand to your feet, bob your head, wave your hands, shake what you momma gave you, and enjoy these lyrics.

"The Other Woman"

CHORUS

Don't let uh Katrina Come between ya—the other woman
Don't let uh Katrina Come between ya—the other woman
Don't let uh Katrina Come between ya—the other woman

VERSE 1

In da garden, Man found none suitable,
but with Yahweh, all things are do-a-ble
He was a yawning, before a rib was taken from his side,
It was a dawning, dat God was making Adam his bride
This is da reason, a man leaving his parents is no treason,
In due season, a man cleaving to his wife to God is pleasing
The two are joined, in what is known as marriage,

GOSPEL CONVERSATIONAL MARRIAGE

And God has coined, what is known as His message
What God designed, let-not-man-redefine
The marriage bed, at all times must be undefiled
Don't let the other woman keep you from loving it,
This is God's holy woven in covenant

VERSE 2

2005 thought I was living, "Husbands love ya wives"
2 weeks into our time at Hebron,
Heard about Katrina started asking "where she-from?"
She blew through with winds & rain of devastation
Closest Tonya and I came to a separation
I spent my time as a minister to those in strife
All da while becoming a visitor to my wife
The other woman dat came between us was a hurricane,
Damage done in our marriage, it was all the same,
God said in da aftermath of those tornadoes
Marriage is a path, not a game using play-doh
So husband & wife should prepare for a lot of work,
But don't lose heart because in Christ God's marriage works!

VERSE 3

Da secret to holy-ever-after has been given us
As we listen to the sequel given by Jesus
Da haters asking Jesus for divorce "just because"
But male & female becoming one was God's just cause
This puzzling union can't be solved by Sherlock Holmes
But it's resolved through wedlock in da home
The Apostle Paul wrote much about this mystery,
Christ and His church, dat is the Gospel, for all to see
My favorite part of dat wedding ceremony
Is when da groom comes down & gets his bride-to-be

It's not a picture of what comes back from a google search,
But it's a picture of God coming back for His church!

CHORUS

Don't let uh Katrina Come between ya—the other woman
Don't let uh Katrina Come between ya—the other woman
Don't let uh Katrina Come between ya—the other woman

I am so thankful to have a wife willing to work, fight, claw, and scratch for our marriage. Husbands and wives, work for your marriage. Is it work? Yes. But it works! God has taught me through His Word that Tonya is my ministry.

Stay in the Word in your home, until your home stays in the Word.

Husbands, Wash Her with the Word

As a pastor, God has reminded me that there will always be another church to pastor, but there is only one wife and one family for me. A heavy and strong word to husbands is given in Ephesians 5:25-26:

Husbands, love your wives, as Christ loved the church and gave himself up for her, that he might sanctify her, having cleansed her by the washing of water with the word.

Husbands, it's our responsibility to make sure our wives are being washed with the Word. As the spiritual leaders, we must have our family in a local church sitting under the teaching and preaching of the Word. Make sure you hold your wife accountable for studying the Word on her own. You and your wife don't have to do daily quiet times together, but you better make sure she is in the Word. Guess what, you can't hold her accountable to being in the Word if you are not. Husbands, the best thing you can do for your marriage is stay in the Word. Stay in the Word in your home, until your home stays in the Word.

Kevin's Story

Is your marriage losing ground? Do you feel like you and your spouse are on the verge of the "D" word? Tonya and I had to deal with the "C" word in marriage, but we vowed to never even use the "D" word in conversation. Just. Not. An. Option. For. Us. Surely, God would never call Tonya and I into the pastorate and then let it all end in the "D" word. Maybe we were naïve thinking this never happens to pastors and pastors' wives. When we heard about Kevin and his wife, we were devastated. Kevin is my friend who happens to be a pastor. Kevin is still a pastor, but he is almost no longer a husband. My heart breaks for my friend.

Per Kevin, the separation from his wife felt like death because their marriage was dying. He went through all the stages of grief. Kevin hit rock bottom, but God didn't leave him there. The Holy Spirit comforted and convicted him all at the same time. As I listened to him share, the Holy Spirit convicted me. God told Kevin that *he failed to wash his wife in the Word.* Ouch. That hurts. Kevin said it was a gradual fade. It happened over time. There were signs along the way that he missed and/or dismissed. His wife began to listen to a lady who was a self-proclaimed prophet. She told Kevin's wife that she was the pastor and not her husband. Pray for Kevin and his wife. Pray that God will restore what Satan has sought to destroy. Pray for repentance. Pray for restoration. Husbands and wives, we must start praying over marriages for we know that Satan is preying on them. Start praying over your own marriage for you know Satan is preying on it.

How you treat your spouse will determine how your adult children treat marriage.

As an American dad to American daughters, I've often wondered if we could adopt the Eastern tradition of arranged marriages. I've got to be honest. The thought of Tonya and I selecting who Braydee and Belle will marry is somewhat appealing. Too many knuckleheads out there, right!? Besides, we know several married couples from India whose marriages were arranged, and they seem to be doing well. Married couples, the truth is we do have more influence over who our children will marry than we think. How you treat your spouse will determine how your adult children treat marriage. Those young eyes are watching you. They are watching how you treat one another, greet one another, love one another, serve one another, forgive one another, talk about one another, talk to one another, fuss with one another, make a fuss over one another, and encourage one another.

Malachi on Marriage

His palms were sweaty. He was holding the ring. His heart was beating at a rapid pace. The young man was proposing to his girlfriend when he said:

"Sweetheart, I love you so much, I want you to marry me. I don't have a car like Johnny Green. I don't have a yacht like him or a house as big as his. I don't have the money of Johnny Green, but I love you with all my heart."

She looked into his eyes and said:

"I love you too, sweetheart...but could you tell me more about Johnny Green?"[lxviii]

Oh, we get distracted so easily. We lose focus in our marriage relationship by giving more attention to all the *Johnny Greens* who look *greener* on the other side.

In Malachi 2:11-16, the minor prophet majorly addressed this age-old problem of making a mockery of marriage:

For Judah has profaned the sanctuary of the LORD, which he loves, and has married the daughter of a foreign god. May the LORD cut off from the tents of Jacob any descendant of the man who does this, who brings an offering to the LORD of hosts! And this second thing you do. You cover the LORD's altar with tears, with weeping and groaning because he no longer regards the offering or accepts it with favor from your hand. But you say, 'Why does he not?' Because the LORD was witness between you and the wife of your youth, to whom you have been faithless, though she is your companion and your wife by covenant. Did he not make them one, with a portion of the Spirit in their union? And what was the one God seeking? Godly offspring. So guard yourselves in your spirit, and let none of you be faithless to the wife of your youth. For the man who does not love his wife but divorces her, says the LORD, the God of Israel, covers his garment with violence, says the LORD of hosts. So guard yourselves in your spirit, and do not be faithless.

Malachi ain't messing around when it comes to marriage.

When Judah returned from captivity, there were some sexy strangers, foreign foxes, heathen hotties, and Baal beauties that the men of Judah desired. Many of these men divorced their wives and *married* these women. The word for *marry* used in Malachi 2:11 is *Baal* in Hebrew, which means *to have dominion over, to possess, take possession of*. How unsettling! *Baal* represents false gods, false religion, evil, wickedness, and Satan himself. Think about that! God's Word calls a spade a spade. A man divorcing his wife for another woman is said to *Baal* himself to the other woman. No thank you! I don't want none of that! I will stay as far away from that as possible! Yet, far too many men are being seduced by Facebook foxes, sexy strangers on social media, instant hook-ups on Instagram, and following old girlfriends on Twitter. Men, don't do it.

Our American view of singleness is too low, while the biblical view of singleness is much higher.

Singles, Don't Settle

Shout-out to the singles! Singleness is not second-class. Singleness is not second-rate. Singleness is not in second-place. Singleness is not a sin. Our American view of singleness is too low, while the biblical view of singleness is much higher. Paul the apostle made the case for a high view of singleness in 1 Corinthians 7:8 and 32-34:

> *To the unmarried and the widows I say that it is good for them to remain single as I am…I want you to be free from anxieties. The unmarried man is anxious about the things of the Lord, how to please the Lord. But the married man is anxious about worldly things, how to please his wife, and his interests are divided. And the unmarried woman or betrothed woman is anxious about the things of the Lord, how to be holy in body and spirit. But the married woman is anxious about worldly things, how to please her husband.*

Singleness is a gift from God and comes with benefits.

First, a single who is following Christ is able to give undivided focus to the Lord Jesus and His kingdom. He or she isn't bound to the responsibilities that accompany husband and wife in marriage. God uses both marriage and singleness to bring about His glory.

Second, unmarrieds are not in ungodly marriages. Some marrieds are in terrible, ungodly marriages. Some believers are unequally yoked, and their marriages are not in a good place. Singles, there is nothing wrong with wanting to be married, but there is something wrong with settling for one who is not a follower of Jesus Christ. Don't do it. One might say *they can convert him or her to Christ*—this is known as *missionary dating*. Missionary dating doesn't work. Singles, *flirt to convert doesn't work*!

Third, singleness affords other relationships in a single's life to flourish. The opportunity to be a great friend, a great brother or sister, a great uncle or aunt, a great son or daughter, a great servant, or a great fellow partner in the gospel increases greatly when one is single. You have more time and opportunity to pour into other relationships when single. A higher view of singleness is necessary for a healthier view of marriage.

The Divine on Divorce

God hates divorce. *Hate* is such a strong word. When we think of God, we think of love, not hate. The reason God hates divorce is because divorce severs a covenant made between a husband and a wife. As much as we try, we can't sugarcoat the fact that God hates divorce. It's not okay to say that God is okay with divorce.

God loves divorced people. God is love. God loves you. God loves you whether you are divorced or not. A bride and groom don't stand at the altar and long for the day they will sign divorce papers. Many people are suffering from the incredible pain of divorce. Whatever brought about your divorce, you need to know that God doesn't hate you. God loves you.

God permits some divorce. God hates all divorce, but He doesn't forbid all divorce. In the restrictive cases of adultery, abandonment, or abuse, the one who was wronged is not obligated to remain married. Concerning the debate over whether abuse is grounds for divorce, Rick Watt wrote:

> The Scriptures assume divorce's reality (Deuteronomy 24:1-4), and all Jews accepted that it was legal; they debated only its grounds. Everyone agreed that adultery and other similarly weighty offenses—e.g. abuse, cruelty, humiliation, persistent refusal to provide requisite food or clothing, willful conjugal or emotional neglect (cf. Exodus 21:10-11)—were clear cause for divorce and required the punishment of the offending party.[lxix]

Though divorce is permitted in strict cases, God is for the restoration of marriage through reconciliation.

I am not Dr. Phil. Tonya likes Dr. Phil's advice. I hear Dr. Phil's advice from Tonya. I am not Dr. Phil. Tonya and I don't have the perfect marriage. Tonya and I are not perfect. The only person who will tell you that I am perfect is Tonya. Of course, right!? Tonya and I have not gone through what you have gone through, and we don't pretend otherwise. We are just two imperfect people following Christ and encourage you to do the same. We both recognize that local churches have failed many people in many ways. The church is not always a place where divorced people feel loved and find healing. As a pastor, I apologize to you for that.

Abuse Is Never Acceptable

Abuse is never acceptable and always unacceptable. The statistics are scary. On average, nearly twenty people per minute are physically abused by an intimate partner in the United States. One in four women, 25%, experience sever intimate partner physical violence or sexual violence in America.[lxx] God intended marriage to be the safest place on earth for a man and a woman. Satan desires for marriage to be the most dangerous place on earth for a man and a woman. God loves you. Satan hates you.

Have you been abused? If so, where do you go from here? First, turn to Jesus. Satan will seek to destroy you by blaming you and then shaming you. He wants you to take responsibility for the abuse that happened to you. Satan would love nothing more than for you to live under that shame. Jesus loves you. Jesus cares for you. Jesus wants you to know that what happened to you was not your fault. Jesus went to the cross to die for all blame and shame. Second, talk to somebody about your abuse. Don't carry this on your own. Reach out. Get help.

Social Media and Marriage

Letter writing was the social media of the day in the first century. John, the disciple whom Jesus loved, was for social media in his day as he wrote five New Testament letters. Yet, John knew the importance and value of face to face conversations:

Though I have much to write to you, I would rather not use paper or ink. Instead I hope to come to you and talk face to face, so that our joy may be complete. 2 John 12

John understood there are times when communication via feather pen to feather pen, fountain pen to fountain pen, Facebook to Facebook, text to text, social media to social media, Twitter to Twitter, or Instagram to Instagram may be appropriate. At the same time, he longed to talk face to face. Social media is here to stay. We must learn to live with it and use it for God's glory. How can we ensure that our time on social media is appropriate?

Social media can be helpful, but it can also be hurtful. What is the effect of social media on marriage? The effect of social media on marriage is real. A third of all divorce filings contain the word "Facebook". What's more, a great number of these filings use posts or messages to make a case for divorce by pointing out a spouse's behavior online. Conversations are happening online. Be sure that in your marriage you and your spouse have some healthy boundaries established.

Don't post what you wouldn't say. Stop posting messages that you wouldn't say with your spouse standing right beside you. Before you hit send, let your spouse read what you are about to send. You need accountability in your social media usage. Your spouse is the best accountability partner on the planet.

Don't air your dirty laundry online. Please. Stop. It. This drives me nuts. For real. I can't even. Build up your spouse all the time. Don't tear them down at any time, especially online. Take the time to sit down and have a face to face conversation with your spouse about any issues in your marriage. Don't let the world in.

Pass on your passwords. Don't pass on passing-on your passwords to your spouse. Not only does Tonya have my passwords, she sets my passwords. She knows passwords on filters for my devices that I don't even know. Don't hide your passwords from your spouse. You and your spouse need to have full access to one another's social media profiles and platforms.

You don't have to hit send. Just because a thought enters your mind doesn't mean it has to exit your mouth. Just because a thought is shared with you doesn't mean you have to share it online. Just because something is *in the secular media* doesn't mean it has to be *on your social media*. It is okay if you don't have an opinion on everything and it is okay if you don't share an opinion on everything.

Social media is tone deaf.

Don't make it about you. Nothing in God's kingdom is about you. Don't make social media about you. Use social media to praise

Jesus and encourage others. Post about the Lord Jesus, your wife, children, family, church, work, and anything else besides yourself. Making social media about you doesn't look good on you.

Watch your tone. Being a dad of daughters comes with a ton of blessings and just a few challenges. Tonya reminds me often to watch my tone. Tone is so important in verbal communication. What we say is important, but how we say what we say is critical. Social media is tone deaf. It is nearly impossible to read someone's tone on social media—especially when one doesn't know how to use emojis appropriately. Guilty. There are just so many emojis to choose from, you know?

You don't have a right to be liked. Husbands and wives, you don't have a right to be liked on social media, but you do have the responsibility to love your spouse. Husbands, the Lord Jesus will not reward you based on how many likes you had on social media, but He will reward you on how you loved your wife. Forfeit your right to be liked on social media for the sake of loving your spouse.

Accountability doesn't happen by accident. Tonya receives an email each time I search or send anything that is questionable. She has access to all my devices. She has access to all my social media outlets. Ask your spouse and one other person to hold you accountable.

Be patient with him or her *on their phones*. Every Sunday I look out from the platform and see church members *on their phones* as we worship. Fellow church members have even let it be known that some people are *on their phones*. Of those who are *on their phones*, some of them are looking up or looking at the Scripture for the sermon that day. No, I am not so naïve to think that none of them are playing on their phones, but some are using their phones for worship. What I am trying to convey is we should be patient with one another.

I am learning this in my own marriage. Tonya is often on her phone working or ministering to other people. Does this mean that we shouldn't limit our time on our devices? No. But, it also doesn't mean that we shouldn't be patient with one another. Certain things Tonya is passionate about on social media, I am not so passionate about—and vice versa. At times in our marriage, Tonya has been more spiritually mature than I have been—and vice versa. When it comes to our faith, there are times when Tonya exercises stronger faith than me—and vice versa. One pastor made a strong point about faith in a sermon clip I recently watched online:

> Picture two Jewish men, the day before the first Passover, talking. And one says to the other:
>
> Are you a little nervous about what is going to happen tonight?
>
> The other one said:
>
> God told us what to do through his servant Moses. There is no reason to be nervous. Haven't you slaughtered the lamb and put the blood on your doorpost? Aren't you going to eat the whole Passover meal with your family?
>
> The first replied:
>
> Of course, I've done all that. I am not stupid. But it's still scary with all that has happened with the flies and the river turning to blood. Just awful. And now there is a threat of the firstborn being killed. It's alright for you. You have three sons, but I only have one. I love my Charlie, and the death angel is passing over tonight. I know what God says, and I put the blood there. But it's still scary, and I'll be glad when this night is over.
>
> The second said:
>
> Bring it on! I trust in the promises of God!

That night the angel of death passed over the land. Which one of these Jewish men lost their son? The answer, of course, is neither. Because death didn't pass over them on the basis of the intensity of the clarity of the faith exercised, but on the basis of the blood of the lamb.[lxxi]

Praise the Lord for the blood of the Lamb! Praise the Lord that the weakness or the strength of faith exercised is not what saves, but it is the blood of the Lamb. Be gracious with one another. Be conversational with one another.

She Says

I joined Facebook in its early stages around twelvish years ago. It was amazing to see all the old friends on there I hadn't seen in years. I remember being pregnant with Belle and I believe one of my first posts was when we were getting ready to head to the hospital to have her.

Braydee and Belle were both born in south Louisiana. They consider themselves Tennessee girls but really, they were born Cajuns. Our time in south Louisiana was hard. Very hard. As Sam mentioned, he was devoted to the other woman in our lives. We had some hard lessons to learn about boundaries with the other woman because Sam was not only fully devoted to the other woman, but he was also a full-time student at the New Orleans Baptist Theological Seminary. And he refused to make anything but an A. So, when second baby came around, it was HARD. I tell Belle all the time that if she'd been the first born, she would be an only child. Braydee kind of tricked us by making us think we had the parenting thing down, so we made the leap and had her a sibling.

Belle humbled us in many ways. She was not an easy child. She cried a lot, never liked being held, wouldn't sleep, and got so impatient once while I was changing her that she dove headfirst off the changing table. I screamed thinking she'd probably broken her neck. But she didn't. She just crawled away butt naked back to Braydee's room where they were having a dandy time before I interrupted.

Between school and the church, Sam was gone a lot and family was hours away. I was struggling. I remember it happening. On my birthday. I got a message on Facebook from an old boyfriend wishing me a happy birthday. I got VERY uncomfortable. I knew I probably shouldn't have even accepted his friend request. I said, "Thank you" and planned for that to be the end of it. But he responded again. I don't even remember what he said, but I immediately UN friended him. That was the end of that. I don't believe the option to block people existed yet but if it had, I'd have done that instead.

Thing is, Satan is crafty, and he can use our vulnerabilities against us. In my loneliness, I could have easily gotten myself into a mess. Men and women do it all the time. Be on guard. John 10:10 tells us,

The thief comes only to steal and kill and destroy. I came that they may have life and have it abundantly.

This thief, Satan, is out to ruin us. He loves it. And he's very smart. A snake in the grass. We have got to be on guard. I am not immune, and you are not immune. None of us are. As soon as we think we are, we are in the most danger. He wants to destroy our marriages and our families, and he will do anything to make it happen.

Braydee once asked me if I checked her dad's phone. Where I watched too much Beverly Hills 90210, she has her Gossip Girl. If you aren't familiar with those shows, everyone cheats on everyone and no one trusts anyone. Ew. Who wants to live like that? But it did remind me of the days when I did think like that. When Sam was roommates with Robert, before we got engaged, I would sneak into his kitchen and check his caller ID to see who'd called him. Yes, I did. When you looked up the word insecure in those days, my picture was right there. Thank God He doesn't leave us where we are.

But I know many women who live like that. Your man has given you all kinds of reasons to not trust him and left you a paranoid, insecure, untrusting hot mess. You don't think you'll ever be able to trust him again. I'm here to tell you God is enough. It took me a long time to come out of it, but once I met Jesus and realized He was the only one who could fill that void, it was all over. I finally realized Sam could never have said all the right things, done all the right things, or been enough to heal me. Only God. And He can do it for you. So, set your husband free from being your savior. He can't do it. No matter how hard he tries, he will fail you. Yes, you can trust him again, and yes, he can be redeemed. I'm here to tell you, God can do anything. Give him a chance. Same for the fellas. You can trust her again, and she is redeemable.

In our house, we all share passwords. Anyone can access anyone's device in our house. Our girls could care less to look at anything on Sam's or my phone, but it's good for accountability. Braydee's friends even tease her because they know her momma checks her texts. Occasionally they'll text an ugly word and immediately say, "Sorry Mrs. Tonya" because they know I'll see it eventually. So, if you are texting, emailing or messaging something you wouldn't want your husband or kids to read, don't hit send.

A few years ago, I had a dear friend and there were things that just never made sense. I like to see the good and be optimistic in all things, but something was just off. It took me a while to realize what was going on and even after I was pretty sure, I kept watching just to be certain. I debated telling her. She really didn't seem to know. She always blamed herself. He would go weeks without speaking to her. Sometimes months. The closer I got to her, the more I watched her agonize day after day. Finally, I knew I had to tell her. I couldn't watch her torment herself anymore. Her self-esteem was on the floor and he let her think low of herself. I didn't plan it. It just came out. "Your husband is abusing you and your children." She had her back turned to me, and immediately she went to the floor and started sobbing uncontrollably. Her whole body shook, and I wondered if I did the right thing. I did not want to ruin her marriage, but I couldn't watch her live like this anymore. I couldn't wait on her to figure it out on her own. She needed someone to tell her the truth.

It was a long and arduous process. They went to counseling, and he did better for a while. Then he had another meltdown, and wouldn't speak for weeks, it would get better and then the whole process would repeat. The secrets started coming out, and it was bad. Worse than I ever imagined. It was a never-ending hamster wheel cycle of better, worse, worser, worsest, worser, worse, better, etc. After exhausting every avenue, she finally left the marriage for the sake of her children and her sanity. She tormented herself, for what seems like years, for going through a divorce as a Christian.

It saddens me that so many live with that shame in the church. Sure, we want to see everyone live a vibrant, happy, fulfilling marriage, but it shouldn't come at the cost of living in abuse. I hate divorce, and I hate that children have to be separated from a parent. I'm a firm believer that kids need both parents in the house. But I'm also aware that on this side of Heaven, there is the need for divorce. I'm happy to say she is doing well and managing all the challenges of being a single mom like a boss. She works HARD. All single parents work hard! It's hard enough being married parents but when you bear the burden on your own, it's a whole new playing field.

All my single ladies (and fellas), do not live in fear and shame. Don't stay home from church because you don't want to go alone. I'm always sitting alone at church and I always invite the single ladies to come sit with me. Find your people. You are not the only one. You may just have to put yourself out there a little to find them but let me tell you, it's so worth it.

Widows, this goes for you too. Our church has way too many ladies who have lost their husbands. I know it's hard, but there are churches with single's and widow's ministries. You are not alone.

Satan wants you to think you are, but get out there. Life here is not over until He returns. So make the best of it!

Sam and I often get questions about marriage and how we've managed to have the one we have after so long. Others see how much fun we have and are curious. So writing a book seemed to make sense. Except I'm not a writer nor am I an expert in all-things-marriage. We've had fun sharing some of our story with you and what works for us. We hope you've enjoyed it and learned something. We don't have any special training on the topic other than being in God's Word and on our knees. We know you can have an amazing marriage, too. Yes, you can!

xoxo

CONVERSATION STARTERS

1. Discuss ways that both you and your spouse can hold one another accountable to being washed in the Word.

2. What guardrails do you have in place to protect one another from the pitfalls of social media usage? Discuss.

3. Discuss areas you need to work on in your use of social media.

4. Read 2 John and discuss what is appropriate and inappropriate as it relates to social media usage.

End Notes

[i] Jagged Edge and Rev Run-DMC, *Let's Get Married.* https://genius.com/Jagged-edge-lets-get-married-remix-lyrics. Accessed 27 February 2021.

[ii] Janet Brito, *64 Terms That Describe Gender Identity and Expression.* https://www.healthline.com/health/different-genders. Accessed 24 March 2021.

[iii] Logos Bible Software. Accessed 10 August 2021.

[iv] Matthew Henry, *Matthew Henry's Commentary on the Whole Bible* (Peabody, MA: Hendrickson Publishers, 2008).

[v] The Dixie Cups, *Chapel of Love.* https://www.azlyrics.com/lyrics/dixiecups/chapelof love.html. Accessed 17 August 2021.

[vi] USA Facts, *The State of American Households: Smaller, More Diverse, and Unmarried.* https://www.usnews.com/news/elections/articles/2020-02-14/the-state-of-american-households-smaller-more-diverse-and-unmarried. Accessed 20 May 2021.

[vii] Jeffery M. Jones, *Is Marriage Becoming Irrelevant.* https://news.gallup.com/poll/316223/fewer-say-important-parents-married.aspx. Accessed 20 May 2021.

[viii] Julian Menasce Horowitz, Nikki Graff and Gretchen Livingston, *The Landscape of Marriage and Cohabitation in the U.S.* https://www.pew

research.org/social-trends/2019/11/06/thelandsca pe-of-marriage-and-cohabitation-in-the-u-s/. Accessed 20 May 2021.

[ix] Brian Hollar, *Regular Church Attenders Marry More and Divorce Less Than Their Less Devout Peers.* https://ifstudies.org/blog/regularchurch-attenders-marry-more-and-divorce-less-than-their-less-devout-peers. Accessed 20 May 2021.

[x] Lisa Bonos, *The Washington Post.* https://www.washingtonpost.com/lifestyle/2021/05/04/gates-divorce-bill-melinda-marriage/. Accessed 29 May 2021.

[xi] John Piper, *"Husbands Who Love Like Christ and the Wives Who Submit to Them,"* sermon preached at Bethel Baptist Church (6/11/08). Accessed 2 June 2021.

[xii] Tim Keller, Twiiter, https://twitter.com/timkellernyc/status/1397554116495347721. Accessed 3 June 2021.

[xiii] Michael Jackson. *Beat It.* https://genius.com/Michael-jackson-beat-it-lyrics. Accessed 17 August 2021.

[xiv] Logos Bible Software. Accessed 15 August 2021.

[xv] Ibid.

[xvi] Edward Davies, *Forget Race of Class, Marriage is the Big Social Divide*, The Spectator. https://www.spectator.co.uk/article/forget-race-or-class-marriage-is-the-big-social-divide. Accessed 5 July 2021.

[xvii] National Abortion Federation, *Women Who Have Abortions.* https://prochoice.org/wpcontent/uploads/women_who_haveabortions.pdf. Accessed 6 July 2021.

[xviii] Ellen Wulfhorst, *Without Family, U.S. Children in Foster Care Easy Prey for Human Traffickers*. https://www.reuters.com/article/us-usa-trafficking-fostercare/without-family-u-s-children-in-foster-care-easy-prey-for-human-traffickers-idUSKBN1I40OM. Accessed 6 July 2021.

[xix] European Commission, *Study on High-Risk Groups for Trafficking in Human Beings*. https://ec.europa.eu/antitrafficking/sites/default/files/study_on_children_as_high_risk_groups_of_trafficking_in_human_beings_-_executive_summary.pdf. Accessed 6 July 2021.

[xx] The Heritage Foundation, *Why the Declining Marriage Rates Affects Everyone*. https://www.heritage.org/marriage-and-family/heritageexplains/why-the-declining-marriage-rate-affects-everyone. Accessed 6 July 2021.

[xxi] Johnny Hunt, Sermon at Men's Night at Red Bank Baptist Church.

[xxii] Logos Bible Software. Accessed 9 August 2021.

[xxiii] Tom Kuntz, *The World's Funniest Jokes*: NYTimes. https://www.preachingtoday.com/search/?query=tent%20camping&contentFilter=Illustration. Accessed 12 July 2021.

[xxiv] Paul David Tripp, *Forever: Why You Can't Live Without It* (Grand Rapids, MI: Zondervan, 2011), 37-39.

[xxv] Paul David Tripp, "Fill in the Blank" Twitter. https://twitter.com/paultripp/status/1374405585496592384. Accessed 12 July 2021.

[xxvi] Art Rainer, *Why Married Couples Should Have Joint Bank Accounts*. https://www.artrainer.com/post/why-married-couples-should-have-joint-bank-accounts. Accessed 13 July 2021.

[xxvii] Elizabeth Cole, *Money Ruining Marriages in America: A Ramsey Solutions Study*. https://www.ramseysolutions.com/company/newsroom/releases/money-ruining-marriages-in-america. Accessed 13 July 2021.

[xxviii] Ibid.

[xxix] Steve Gaines speaking at a retreat in 2017.

[xxx] Quoted and adapted from an excerpt of a sermon preached by Alistair Begg. https://twitter.com/MattSmethurst/status/14071297493113978188. Accessed 16 July 2021.

[xxxi] Wink News, *LSCO: Lehigh Acres groom arrested after attacking wedding guests, deputies*. https://www.winknews.com/2021/07/12/lcso-lehigh-acres-groom-arrested-after-attacking-wedding-guests-deputies/#. Accessed 15 July 2021.

[xxxii] Steven Spence, "What Do You Do When the Wine Runs Out." https://sermons.faithlife.com/sermons/108065-what-do-you-do-when-the-wine-runs-out. Accessed 16 July 2021.

[xxxiii] Adapted from Marriage Retreat with Mark and Peggy Hayman.

[xxxiv] Ibid.

[xxxv] Ibid.

[xxxvi] Ibid.

[xxxvii] Ibid.

[xxxviii] Ibid.

[xxxix] Logos Bible Software. Accessed 16 August 2021.

[xl] Paul David Tripp, *6 Types of Grace*. https://www.paultripp.com/articles/posts/6-types-of-grace. Accessed 20 July, 2021.

[xli] Justin Taylor, *The Grace of God in Every Book of the Bible*. https://www.thegospelcoalition.org/blogs/justin-taylor/the-grace-of-god-in-every-book-of-the-bible-2/. Accessed 20 July 2021.

[xlii] Greg Smalley, *Giving Your Spouse Grace*. https://www.focusonthefamily.com/marriage/giving-your-spouse-grace/. Accessed 20 July 2021.

[xliii] Ray Ortlund, *Who are you married to? https://www.thegospelcoalition.org/blogs/ray-ortlund/who-are-you-married-to/*. Accessed 20 July 2021.

[xliv] Ed Young Jr, *Pastor's Advice for Better Marriage: More Sex*. https://www.nytimes.com/2008/11/24/us/24sex.html

[xlv] Chuck Herring, *Serving Your Spouse*. Sermon preached at Collierville FBC on September 2, 2012. https://assets.speakcdn.com/assets/2426/9-2-12am.pdf. Accessed 21 July 2021.

[xlvi] William F. Harley, *His Needs, Her Needs: Building a Marriage that Lasts.* (Ada, MI: Baker Publishing Group, 2020).

[xlvii] Matthew Henry, *Matthew Henry's Commentary on the Whole Bible* (Peabody, MA: Hendrickson Publishers, 2008), Luke 20.

[xlviii] The Babylon Bee, *New Atheist Chick-fi-A Competitor Only Open on Sundays*. https://babylonbee.com/news/new-atheist-chick-fil-a-competitor-only-open-on-Sundays. Accessed 19 July 2021.

[xlix] Prince. 1999. https://www.azlyrics.com/lyrics/prince/1999.html. Accessed 18 August 2021.

[l] Tony Evans, Twitter, https://twitter.com/drtonyevans/status/307280735604195328?lang=en. Accessed 23 July 2021.

[li] Rick Bentley, *Why is "This Is Us' so popular? The answer is simple*. https://www.seattletimes.com/entertainment/tv/why-is-this-is-us-so-popular-the-answer-is-simple/. Accessed 23 July 2021.

[lii] Douglas O' Donnell. *The Song of Solomon*. (Wheaton, IL: Crossway, 2012), 72-73.

[liii] Tim Keller, *The Meaning of Marriage: Facing the Complexities of Commitment with the Wisdom of God* (New York, NY: Riverhead Books, 2011), 257.

[liv] C.S. Lewis, *Mere Christianity*. https://www.enotes.com/homework-help/what-c-s-lewis-saying-casual-sex-following-passage-325997. Accessed 28 July 2021.

[lv] The Wedding Report, *2020 Covid-19 Wedding Market Impact*. https://wedding.report/index.cfm/action/blog/view/post/pid/1490/title/2020_Covid_19_Wedding_Market_Impact. Accessed 29 July 2021.

[lvi] Ray Ortlund. *Marriage and the Mystery of the Gospel*. (Wheaton, IL: Crossway, 2016), 65.

[lvii] David George Moore and Daniel L. Akin. *Holman Old Testament Commentary: Ecclesiastes and Song of Songs*. (Nashville, TN: Broadman and Holman Publishers, 2003), 252.

[lviii] Merriam-Webster, *body- shaming definition*. https://www.merriam-webster.com/dictionary/webster.com/dictionary /body-shaming. Accessed 29 July 2021.

[lix] Keller, 253.

[lx] Ibid., 268.

[lxi] Ed Young Sr, *Pastor's Advice for Better Marriage: More Sex*. https://www.nytimes.com/2008/11/24/us/24sex.html. Accessed 29 July 2021.

[lxii] Ibid.

[lxiii] Tonya Greer, "My Baggy Red Sweats."

[lxiv] Clan Stubbs, *Sex and the Gospel*. https://cobirmingham.org/blog/2019/08/22/sex-and-the-gospel. Accessed 29 July 2021.

[lxv] Logos Bible Software. Accessed 17 August 2021.

[lxvi] Tony Evans, Twitter. https://twitter.com/drtonyevans/status/1421512764703580161. Accessed 31 July 2021.

[lxvii] John MacArthur, *The MacArthur New Testament Commentary: Hebrews* (Chicago, IL: Moody Publishers, 1983), 134.

[lxviii] Ray Pritchard, *Making a Marathon Marriage*. https://www. Keepbelieving.com/sermon/ 2003-05-18-making-a-marathon-marriage/ Accessed 12 August 2021.

[lxix] Joshua Sharp, *Voices: Abuse is biblical grounds for divorce.* https://www.baptiststandard.com/opinion/voices/abuse-is-biblical-grounds-for-divorce/. Accessed 16 August 2021.

[lxx] National Statistics Domestic Violence Fact Sheets. https://ncadv.org/STATISTICS. Accessed 16 August 2021.

[lxxi] Twitter. https://twitter.com/RRuiz1689/status/1419032340739723265. Accessed 16 August 2021.

GOSPEL CONVERSATIONAL MARRIAGE

GOSPEL CONVERSATIONS
WITH SAM GREER

RESOURCES

In his books, *The Gospel Conversation, The Gospel Conversationalist,* and *The Gospel Conversational Church,* Sam Greer provides a biblical, intentional, and practical approach to engaging the lost in everyday life. Buy your copies today at **gsplconversations.org/books**.

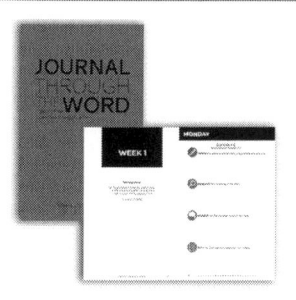

1% of your time can affect 100% of your life! Bible studies are great, but studying the Bible is life-changing! The Bible is not merely a good book, it is God's book. Take the journey of journaling through the Bible. Allow God to stretch you, grow you, and bless you as you journal through the Word. More info at **gsplconversations.org**.

Download the **Our Family Tree** evangelism app. This tool provides a simple framework to share the gospel with anyone, anywhere, at anytime! Download the app today in the App Store or on Google Play.

Follow Sam Greer on Twitter.
@SamGreer_PSG

Scan Here to book Sam to speak.

Made in the USA
Columbia, SC
25 March 2025